Art and Crafts From Other Times
The History of Man Through Art

written and illustrated by
Judy Hierstein

FS-10210 Art and Crafts From Other Times
All rights reserved–Printed in the U.S.A.
Copyright © 1996 Frank Schaffer Publications
23740 Hawthorne Blvd.
Torrance, CA 90505

To the Teacher

This book has been designed to provide the classroom teacher with ideas to enrich his or her study of history with art ideas and projects that simulate the crafts from various historical periods.

History, of course, involves much more than crafts. Still, the art and crafts produced during a particular historical period can tell us much about the people. The earliest-known art comes from the earliest-known people—prehistoric humans. From evidence such as the paintings on walls of caves and tools and jewelry from burial sites, we can see the importance of hunting, early man's love of beauty and self-adornment, and also reverence for life and death. A flute fashioned from a bird's hollow bone shows us early man's interest in music. Using evidence such as this along with fossil evidence, scientists are able to piece together an ever clearer picture of our ancient predecessors.

The types of art and crafts produced by a people are determined to a certain extent by several factors—their physical and spiritual needs, the demands of their environment, and the materials available from which to fashion objects. These factors are presented briefly in each chapter to provide a greater understanding of the people. The art form is then described and translated into projects appropriate for the middle grade level.

Also included in this book are examples of art that is not visual (such as music, theater, literature, costume, dance, architecture) which reinforce the general attitudes of the people during any given place and time. Great creative minds in one area of the arts often color all the other art forms. The arts not only reflect the thinking of a people, but can also change it.

This book begins with a time line which can be completed gradually as each historical (and prehistorical) period is explored. The art and craft ideas proceed chronologically up to the present. Students are even invited to speculate on the possible directions art will take as the future unfolds. So jump in your time machines, fasten your seat belts, and prepare to go back in time!

You may wish to have your students create a bulletin board display to highlight art and crafts through time. (See the sketch on page iv.) As students complete various projects, add them to the display.

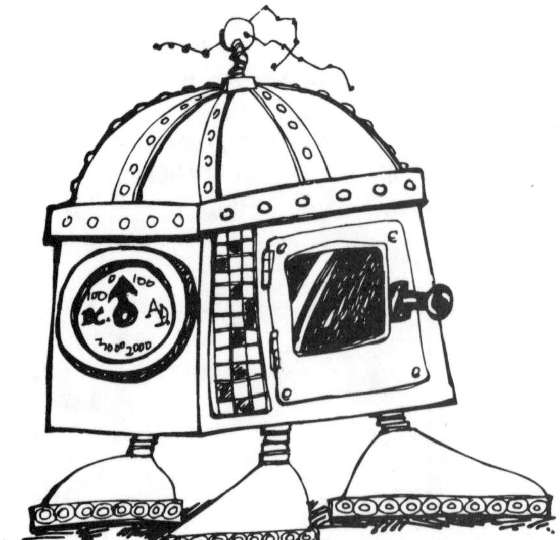

Time Line

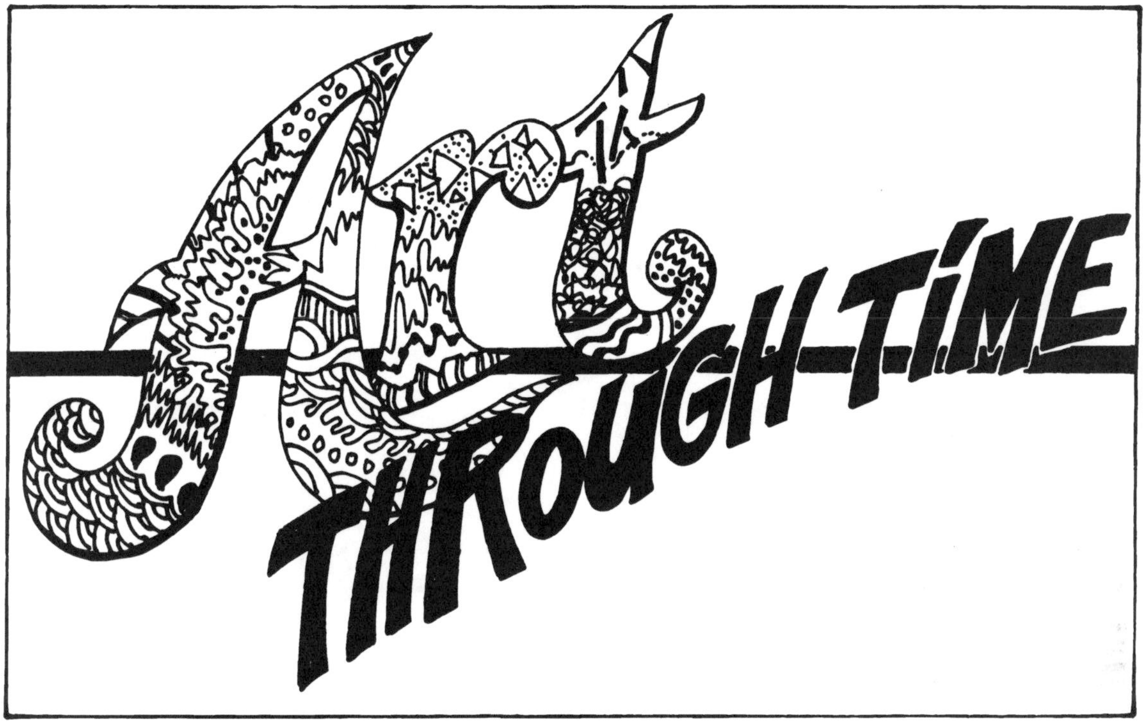
Art
THROUGH TIME

The art and craft ideas in this book progress as history progresses so that students can better see how each successive step in the development of the arts has built on (or reacted to) what has gone before. This concept can be reinforced visually with a time line.

The time line can be as simple or as complicated as time allows, depending on what is included in the year's studies. To create a time line, have students glue a one-inch wide strip of construction paper horizontally across the middle of large sheet of paper. Have them cut out letters to spell "ART THROUGH TIME" by using an interesting print of gift wrap paper for the word "ART" and simple black letters for "THROUGH TIME." Tell students to glue these letters onto the large sheet of paper.

As you study each period from the history of art, have students add the name of the period to the time line using lettering appropriate to the art of that time. A sample lettering style is included at the beginning of each chapter. Once the chapter has been studied and some projects have been completed, students should have no difficulty drawing a tiny version of their art project, cutting it out, and attaching it to the time line to illustrate it. To accompany the small illustration, have students add a brief sentence of explanation. Students may tape additional sheets to the end of the time line as needed.

If time does not permit you to participate in every activity presented, let your class take a whirlwind trip through art history. Have each student, pair, or small group select one of the projects in this book as an outside assignment. Be certain that each project is accompanied by the small drawing as described above to add to a class time line. Assemble the time line and display it as a background to refer to as each project is reported to the class.

Back in Time Bulletin Board

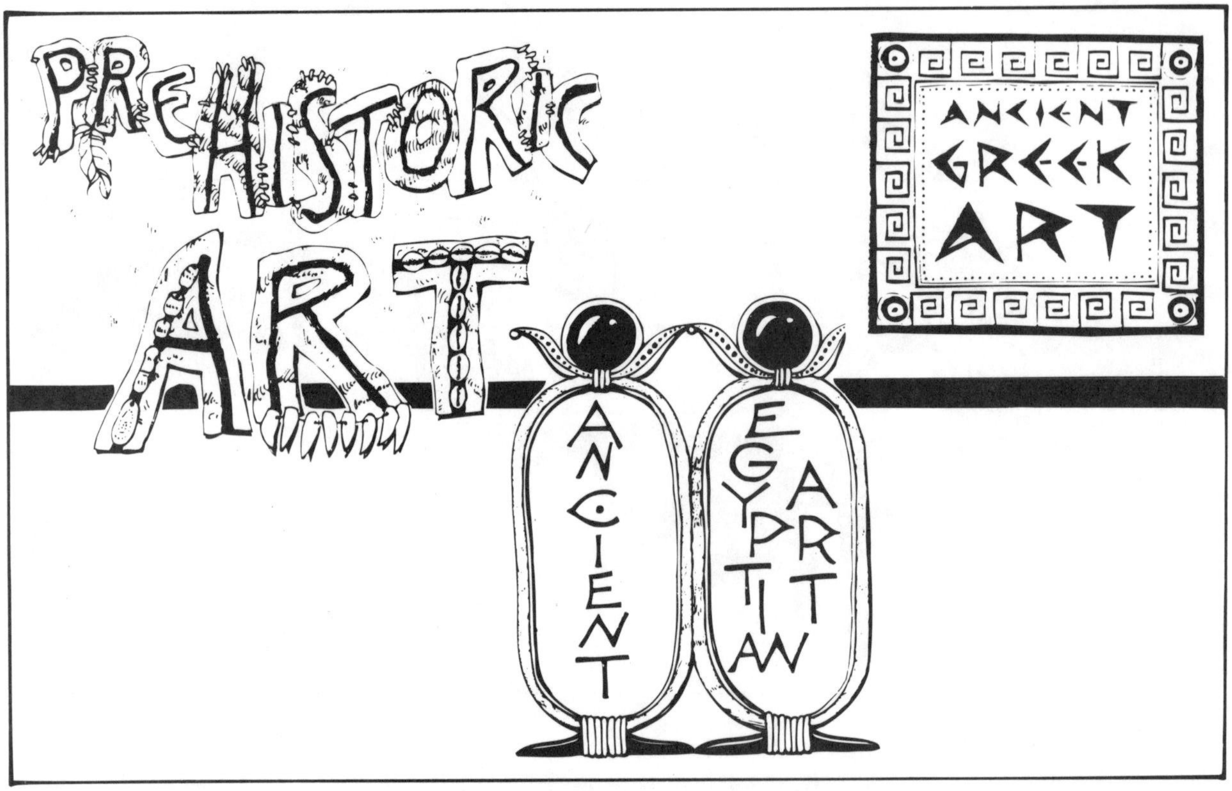
PREHISTORIC ART
ANCIENT GREEK ART
ANCIENT
EGYPTIAN ART

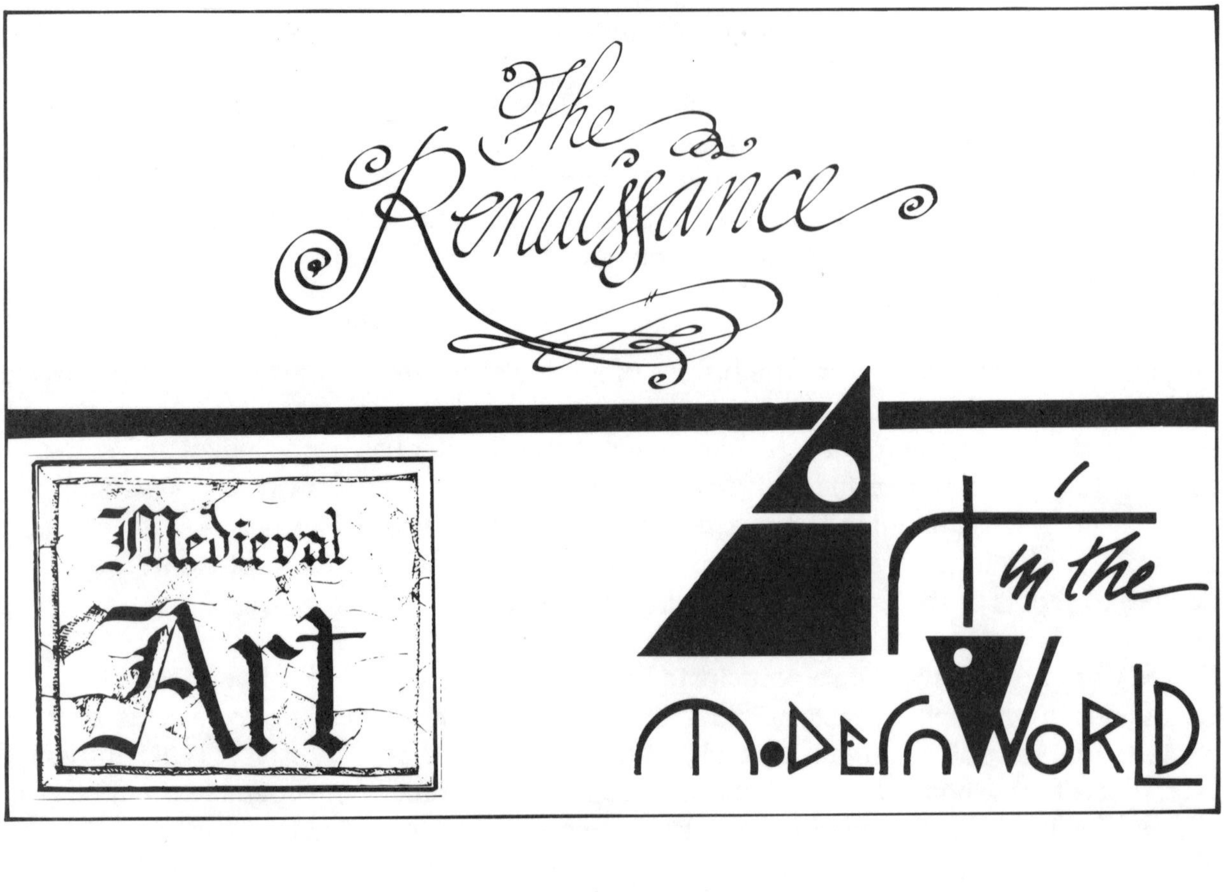
The Renaissance
Medieval Art
Art in the Modern World

Prehistoric Art

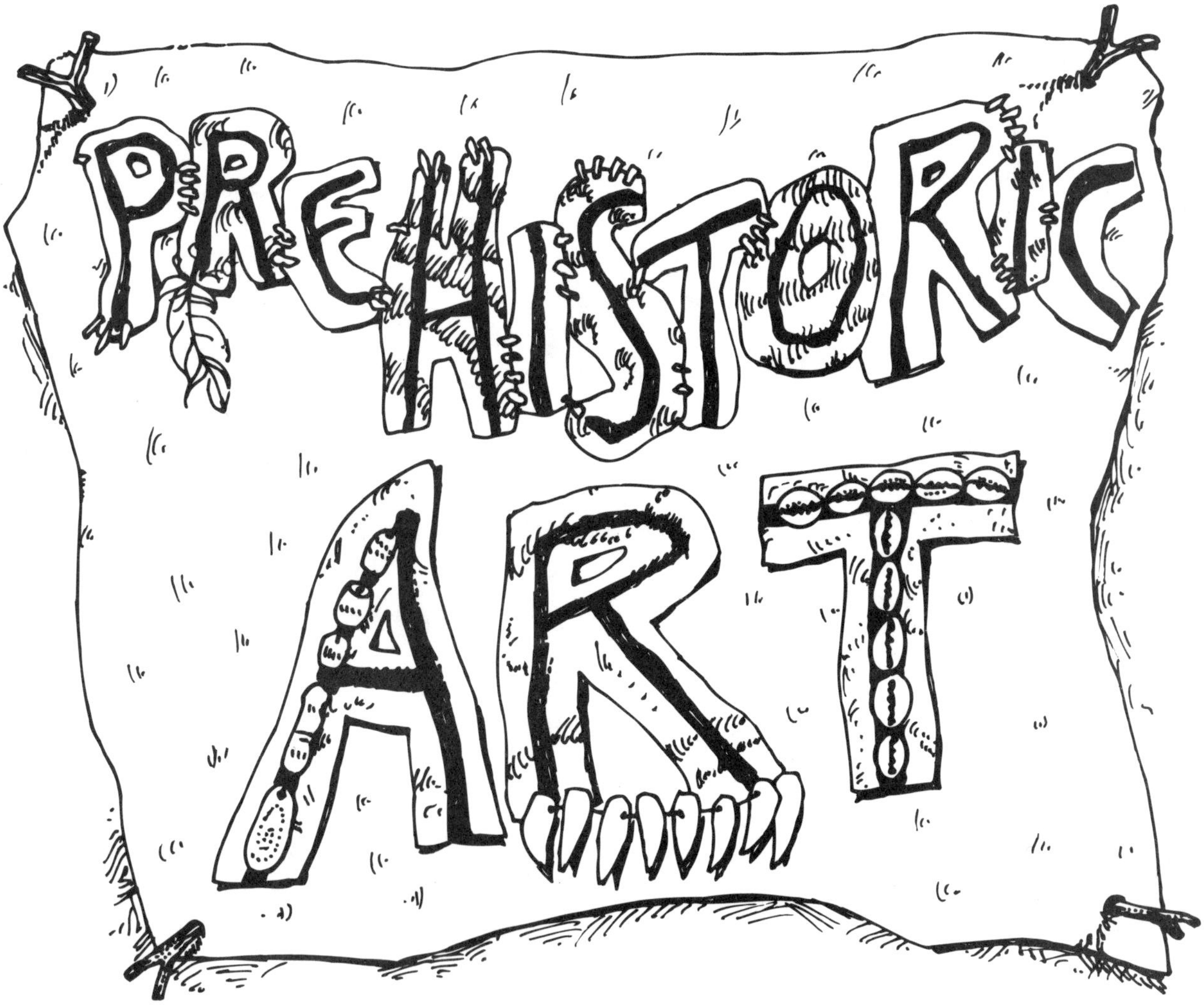
PREHISTORIC
ART

Modern people first appeared on Earth around 40,000 years ago. Like the Neanderthals who preceded them, they lived in groups and cooperated in hunting for food, wore skins of animals, made tools, used fire, knew about herbal medicines, cared for elderly and sick members of his community, and buried the dead with great care. But, unlike the Neanderthals, modern people developed those characteristics that made them unique among the animals—they created music, language, and art.

Prehistoric people possessed the intelligence, imagination, and creative power to make images and symbols to represent elements of their world. This feat has been called the miracle of abstraction, and it marks the beginning of civilization as we know it today.

Old Fashions

Modern prehistoric people wore skins for warmth. They were stretched, scraped, and cut with flint knives, then shaped and stitched using animal tendons, horsehair, or twisted vegetable fibers for "thread." The sewing kits consisted of flint piercers, ivory pins, and even ivory needles with eyes. The practice of wearing clothing set humans apart from other animals. It protected them from the elements and enabled them to survive in harsh climates, thus increasing the areas of Earth in which they were able to live. Human beings spread to virtually every corner of the globe, arriving last in what we now know as the Americas.

Clothing soon took on another purpose, that of self-adornment for beautification. Beautiful skins and furs were especially prized over ordinary ones, and some of them appear to have been painted with ochre and other natural pigments available to these people. Early humans may have begun decorating their bodies with paint at this time—the first makeup!

Activities and Projects

Dress a doll. Study the examples below of early man to become familiar with one type of clothing worn in a chilly climate. Other styles would have been created for warmer climates or summer seasons. Collect scraps of leather, or fabric that resembles leather, and fake fur; leather thongs; shoe laces or heavy thread in earth tones; and an old doll. (If necessary, use heavy brown paper instead of fabric.) Pretend you are a prehistoric person and begin to experiment, piecing scraps together to create clothing that will serve the purposes it must. Will it protect the wearer from the cold? Does it enable him or her to move as he or she must to escape predators, hunt or gather, and carry that which has been foraged? Is it attractive? (Remember, beauty is in the eye of the beholder.) There were no patterns or how-to instructions for the first tailors! Overlap or cut away excess skins and fur, punch holes along the edges of the pieces and lace them together with leather thongs or shoelaces. Wind thongs or laces around the feet and lower legs to hold "shoes" in place. Add pouches to hold totems and medicines, herbs, nuts, grains, berries, etc., that have been gathered while wandering. Add necklaces and other adornments to the clothing, face, and hair. Be creative—the early humans were!

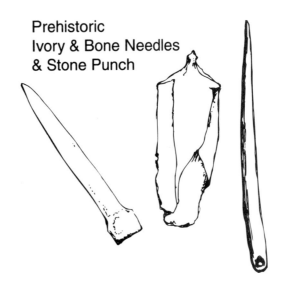

Prehistoric
Ivory & Bone Needles
& Stone Punch

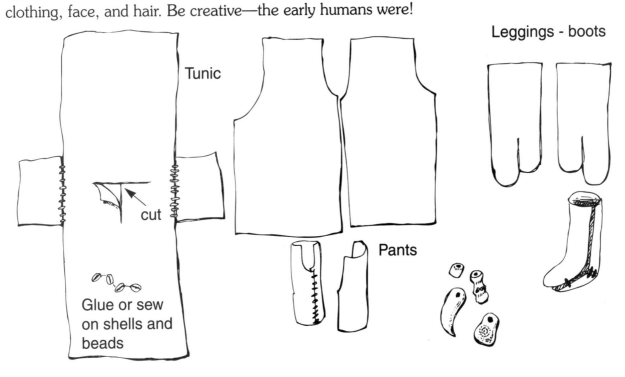

Tunic
cut
Glue or sew on shells and beads
Pants
Leggings - boots

Nature Necklaces

Jewelry was also very common during prehistoric times. Shells and animal teeth were painstakingly pierced and threaded into necklaces, bracelets for upper and lower arms, and pendants. Ivory, bone, and reindeer antlers were carved into beads (which were sometimes sewn directly onto clothing) or pendants of many different shapes such as circles, ovals, rectangles, animals, fish, and birds. Flat bones from shoulder blades and horse's necks were cut into shapes, and drawings were scratched onto them. One particularly beautiful necklace found at a child's burial site in Siberia consists of carved beads and a pendant of an abstract bird in flight dotted with small holes for decoration. Experts feel that birds represent the rebirth which occurs each year with the coming of spring and that they may even have religious significance when placed in a grave as this necklace was.

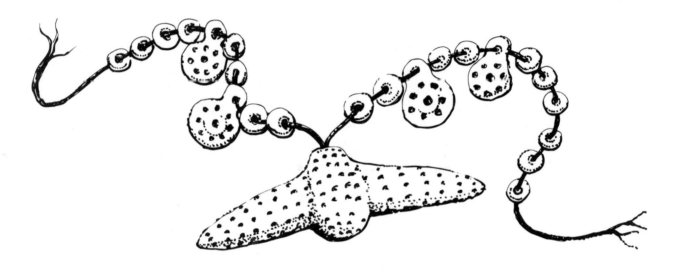

Activities and Projects

Make a nature necklace. First, take a hike. Prehistoric people collected beautiful objects from nature to adorn themselves, so collect anything you come across that is not made by humans, is small in size, and that you feel could adorn a human attractively. Possible items would include acorns or other nuts or seeds, feathers, shells, birch bark, colorful leaves, stones, or moss and lichens. You can even make models of "ivory and bone" saber-tooth tiger teeth, beads, and pendants using creamy white colored sculpture material, or make your own clay by mixing one-half cup of salt, one-quarter cup of flour, and about three tablespoons of water. Keep the clay wrapped in plastic until you are ready to use it. Lay the newly created beads on waxed paper to dry. You may also carve beads and pendants from broken plaster. Mix the plaster, pour it into plastic foam meat trays to about one-half- to three-quarter-inch thickness. Allow it to dry, and then score and break it into pieces. This method is more difficult as the plaster becomes increasingly brittle as it is being worked. It requires patience, as plaster must be slowly scraped into the desired shape. Holes for hanging the pieces must be bored ever so gradually. Finish the pieces by applying a coat of shellac or varnish that has a tiny bit of brown or golden stain added to it. This will create quite durable and authentically old-looking carvings.

Arrange the pieces that have been found or made in the order that they will be placed on the finished piece. Thread the necklace together using a long leather thong, a thin shoelace, natural raffia or fibers, or seine string. A hot glue gun is handy to secure those items which are difficult to bore holes into. (This is not authentic, but to acquire gum glue from tree sap or bison hooves is almost as difficult today as it probably was in prehistoric times!)

Carved Ivory

Probably because they were available, beautifully lustrous, and somewhat easily carved, ivory and bone were used by early people to create a number of different objects. As mentioned previously, they used ivory needles to make clothing and ivory beads and buttons to decorate it. They fashioned spear throwers, staffs, and harpoons from long bones and carved the ends with the heads and bodies of bison, horses, or other animals. Perhaps they believed the carvings enhanced the effectiveness of the tool or weapon if the spirit of the animal was captured within the carved likeness. Perhaps carving the animals simply appealed to early people's aesthetic sense.

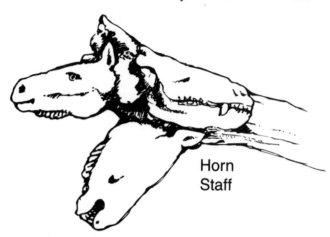

Horn
Staff

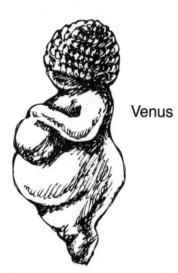

Venus

Many examples of small "Venuses" have also been found carved from ivory and almost every other material. These figures are representations of females, usually faceless. Their plumpness is highly exaggerated as if they are pregnant. Because so much depended on the fertility of the land, the animals, and humans themselves, many scientists believe that these figures represent the idea of life replenishing itself rather than any actual human beings.

Realistic representations of prehistoric people in ivory or bone are much less common, and their rarity puzzles scientists. If carving a representation of an animal was thought to give people power over that beast's spirit, and the Venus figures gave power over the unpredictable world, by the same reasoning, carving a likeness of a person may have been considered too risky. Perhaps it was thought to bring bad luck or loss of power, control, or spirit.

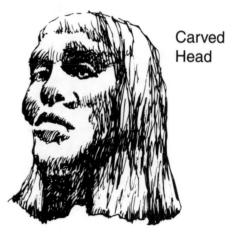

Carved
Head

One rare carving of a lifelike human head, complete with eyelids, pupils, and nostrils, was found in a field in Czechoslovakia in the 1890s and kept in the finder's family until recently, when it was presented to experts for analysis. They were skeptical at first, since microscopic examination often reveals evidence of forgery, but this head appears to be genuine. Dating back 26,000 years, it could be the oldest known portrait of an Ice Age man.

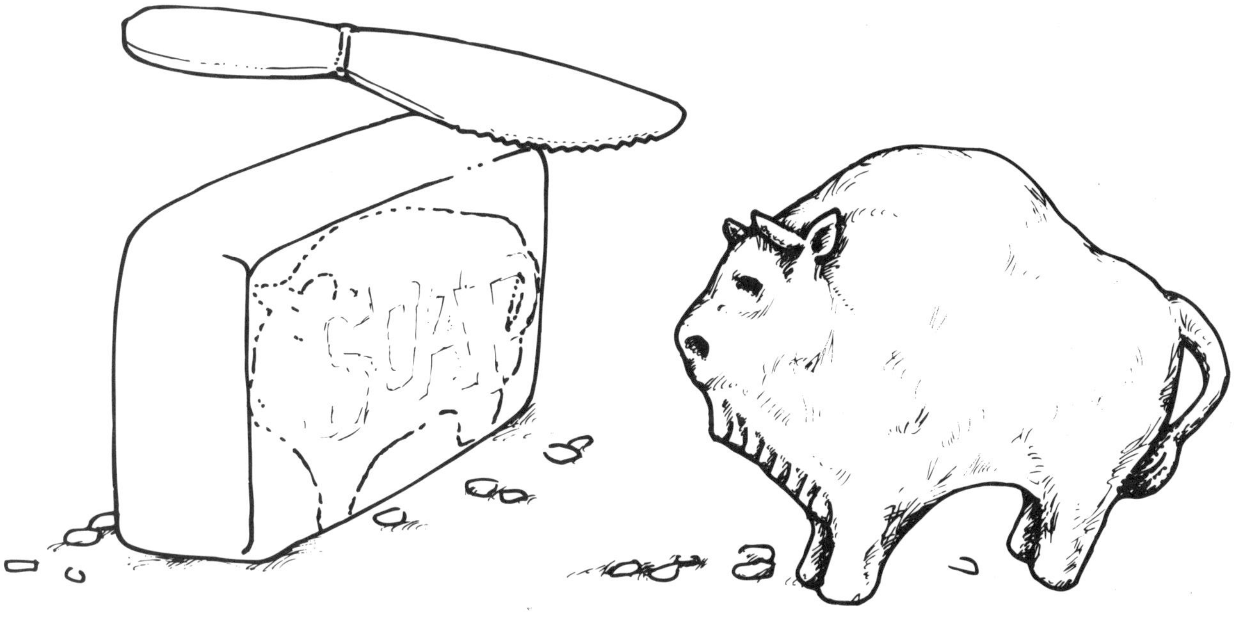
SOAP

Activities and Projects

Carve some ivory (soap, that is). Study some of the examples of carving illustrated here and others you find in your research. You may wish to carve a stylized animal or human, or a realistic one. Make sketches from all sides of the figure you wish to create. Onto the flat side of a bar of ivory-colored soap, scratch the outline of your figure; then gradually begin to scrape away the excess, using a plastic knife, or any clay-carving tool. Turn the piece frequently, working on all sides at the same time. Add details such as hair, fur, or decorative dots and designs with dowels sharpened in a pencil sharpener. When you have finished, make up the story of your creation. Was it carried for good luck? Was it used to hunt animals or fish? Or did you, as a prehistoric human being, simply have a little free time, a spare piece of ivory, and a sharp stone, and almost without thinking discover art?!

Stone and Clay Relief Carvings

In contrast to the small ivory and bone pieces made by prehistoric man, but perhaps with similar significance, were the enormous, sometimes larger than life-sized, stone and clay relief carvings that have been discovered deep inside caves. Early artists usually found a stone formation inside the cave whose natural shape suggested a part of an animal. Then they carved into and around this existing shape to bring out the beast more clearly. For this process the artists used stone tools that had been fashioned by striking them in just the right spots with other stones. Creating the clay figures was much easier, as the clay was wet and soft when these were modeled. A cave discovered in France in 1912, Tuc d'Audoubert, contains two clay bison, male and female. There is also evidence that a smaller bison existed, but it has been removed. These were modeled from a slab of wet clay more than a meter across and are propped up on a rock. Surrounding the beasts are heel prints made in the damp clay by prehistoric youths, perhaps as they performed a ritual dance around the figures.

Clay Bison
in French Cave

Activities and Projects

Model a clay figure. Using a thick slab of clay from the art room or collected along a muddy riverbank, make a relief sculpture of a prehistoric animal. First gouge the outline and carefully remove the excess clay. Then round the edges to create a three-dimensional effect. Scrape away clay on either side of the front leg to make it appear to stand out. Repeat the process to form the ear, the horn, tail, and back haunches. Scratch holes and lines to represent details such as fur and nostrils. These animals were viewed from one side only, so you need not be concerned with the other side. As your creation dries, especially if you have used mud as early man did, it may develop cracks. These will add to its authenticity.

Cave Paintings

Probably the most amazing of all prehistoric art discovered so far are the cave paintings in France and Spain. When the great modern artist Pablo Picasso first saw a cave painting, he was so impressed he declared, "We (artists of today) have invented nothing." While early people sometimes lived under stone overhangs and in the mouths of caves, they painted deep inside the earth in places often accessible only by narrow and mazelike passages. It was pitch black except for undependable torches and a kind of candle made by placing animal fat on a piece of sandstone and adding a wick made of dried plant matter. As with the stone carvings, artists took advantage of the natural bulges in the cave walls to create a more three-dimensional effect in their paintings. Their paint was ground from natural substances and mixed with animal fat or blood to produce ochre, rusty oranges, reds, and black. These pigments were applied with frayed sticks, brushes, or fingers, and some were even blown on by taking the paint into the mouth and spraying it out through a hollow bone.

The best known of these caves are Lascaux in France, dating from 17,000 to 18,000 years ago, and Altamira in Spain, which is thought to have been painted about 12,000 years ago. On their walls are hundreds of aurochs bulls (ancient oxen), horses, and deer, along with mysterious dots and geometric figures. These two caves are not the only ones, however. Over 200 caves with prehistoric art of some kind have been discovered in Europe alone, with a new one unearthed nearly every year. Recently the French government announced the discovery of a Paleolithic cave near Avignon by Jean-Marie Chauvet. It is older than Lascaux or Altamira, dating back 20,000 years. This cave's paintings consist of not only animals that early people hunted, bison and mammoths, but predators as well, such as cave bears, panthers, owls, and hyenas.

Why early people painted on the inner walls of caves remains a mystery, though intelligent guesses have been made. We know that the human brain had developed a large frontal lobe over time. This is where the thinking takes place which allows us to symbolize—the essence of artistic expression. We think painted caves may have been the setting for youth initiation ceremonies, ritualistic preparations for a hunt, or celebrations after a hunt. Most scientists agree that these paintings had great significance, not only because they are so deep inside the caves and difficult to reach, but because, in creating the images on the cave walls, artists were risking their lives.

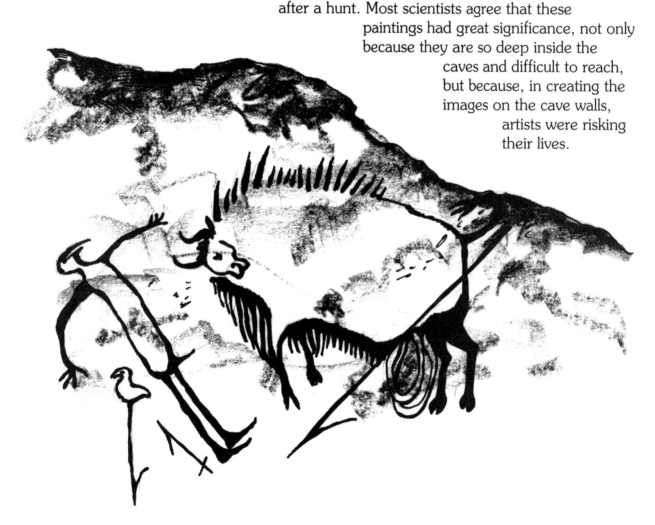

Some of the pigments used (sometimes applied by mouth) were poisonous. Perhaps the shamans (priests) were the artists and this sacrifice was thought to be worth the benefits it brought to the tribe. Those who have had the privilege of viewing these great works of art in the still silence of the inner reaches of Earth compare the feeling to that of being in the sanctuary of a church, temple, or mosque.

Activities and Projects

Create a cave painting. Begin by deciding on the surface and the size. You may know of an outcropping of rock or an actual cave where you could work, or collect a piece of stone that is somewhat flat and small enough to carry. You can create the effect of natural rock by crumpling heavy paper such as the brown paper used for grocery bags. Sometimes large rolls of this stone-colored paper are available. For the "paint," collect bits of charcoal, chalk, and dirt (if rusty colors are available where you live) and grind it to a fine powder using a mortar and pestle. Mix each with water or oil to the consistency of paint and fray the end of a short stick to create a brush. Though authentic, this is a lot of trouble, so you may prefer instead to simply use charcoals and chalk pastels in the earth-tone colors described above. Study the examples of cave painting illustrated here and in your research and decide which beasts hold

particular meaning for you. Then practice a few sketches. Begin your final artwork by outlining the animal with black or brown. Fill in the body, gradually shading the figure to create a feeling of roundness. Many of the bellies of the beasts in the cave are white and fade to the rusty brown of the back. Sometimes animals are drawn one over the other, or hunting scenes are depicted with stylized men throwing spears which have pierced through the skin of the animals. Add the mysterious dots and geometric figures and the signature handprints, but avoid the mouth-spray method of applying the paint!

If your school or town has a large unpainted concrete wall, ask permission to use that surface as a canvas, as long as you use chalk that will wash off the next time it rains. Be certain to photograph the finished work before the first drops fall!

Ancient Egyptian Art

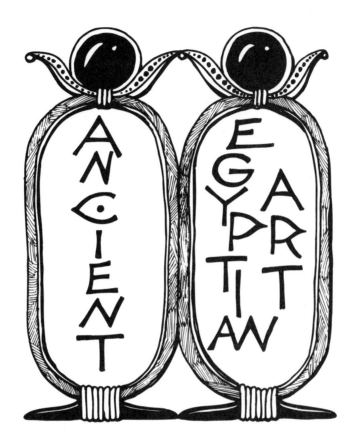

As people learned how to cultivate the land and domesticate animals, their nomadic hunter-gatherer lifestyle disappeared, and they began to live in settlements. With the advent of agriculture, food supplies were more plentiful and people had free time to fashion pottery, weapons, and tools. Learning how to work with copper, bronze, and iron made life even better. People specialized in different occupations, and markets sprang up so people could trade their excess for what they needed. All members of a town had specific duties or jobs, and all had to abide by regulations and laws for the good of all. By that time, society was becoming so complex that a means to keep track of things was necessary— writing. Prehistory was over!

One such settlement was the ancient city called Catal Huyuk. About 8,000 years ago, Catal Huyuk was located in what is now Turkey. It is thought to have been home to nearly 6,000 people. Other settlements were developed in the lands between the Tigris and the Euphrates rivers known as the fertile crescent.

One of the greatest ancient civilizations was Egypt, whose works of art leave us in awe today. The Egyptians were a deeply religious people, and most of the fantastic treasures that remain, even the pyramids, are a part of the elaborate burial customs observed by the pharaohs.

Hieroglyphics

Much of what we know about the ancient Egyptians is written on the walls of the tombs of the pharaohs. The writing is called *hieroglyphics,* a term that comes from two Greek words that mean "sacred writing." These strange, beautiful pictures have long been recognized as writing, but their meaning was not understood until 1822 when a Frenchman named Champollion made a breakthrough in deciphering the hieroglyphics of the Rosetta stone. This stone was found near the mouth of the Nile River near Rosetta, Egypt. It was engraved with the same inscription in three different scripts: Egyptian hieroglyphic, ancient Egyptian demotic, and Greek, which was understood. With the Rosetta Stone as the key and years of work, the mysterious "sacred writing" was finally deciphered.

Hieroglyphics consists of three main types of characters: ideograms, phonograms, and determinatives. The ideograms are simplified pictures of objects drawn to convey the idea of that object. A bird means bird, an eye may mean to see, and so on. A phonogram is like a

rebus. It combines several pictures to comprise syllables of more abstract ideas or feelings. For example, a picture of a bee followed by a leaf would represent the English word "belief." Finally, determinatives were used by ancient Egyptians to indicate the class of object to which the preceding hieroglyphic belonged. For example, the symbol for water would be placed after the name of a specific lake.

Hieroglyphic texts may be read left to right, right to left, or top to bottom, depending on which direction the author/artist felt best fit the space. When several hieroglyphic symbols are encircled in an oval shape, it is called a *cartouche* and it indicates that a name is written inside.

Activities and Projects

Design your own Egyptian cartouche. Study the sample cartouches shown above that were found among the treasures of King Tutankamen's tomb. The basic oval shape in which the name is written in hieroglyphics is adorned with precious and semi-precious stones such as turquoise, lapis lazuli, jasper, carnelian, faience, and amethyst inlaid in gold. Look in an encyclopedia at the hieroglyphic symbols and the corresponding letters of our alphabet. Figure out how your name would be written in Egyptian hieroglyphics. Sketch an oval cartouche shape, add some Egyptian-style designs around it, and write your name inside. Trace or redraw your design onto a flat stone or plaster surface, or onto heavy paper such as an opened grocery bag. Then carefully paint it with tempera paint in colors that match those used in ancient Egypt (white, black, turquoise, royal blue, orange-red, gold).

Mummies and Canopic Jars

The Egyptians believed in an afterlife, and they thought they needed their bodies after they died for the next world. To preserve the body, the Egyptians mummified it using an elaborate process. They first removed the organs and placed them in canopic jars with lids carved like the heads of animals. The lungs, intestines, stomach, and liver were placed in jars that had stoppers shaped like a baboon, falcon, jackal, and man, respectively. The heart remained in the body so it could be weighed by the gods who interrogated the dead person and assessed his good and bad deeds to determine whether or not he was fit for afterlife. The brain, considered worthless, was extracted through the nostrils and discarded. To prevent rotting, the body was then placed in a salt-like substance called *natron* for about 40 days until it was completely dried out. Then it was wrapped in layers of linen.

Activities and Projects

Make a set of canopic jars. Study the canopic jars shown above and then design some of your own. These jars were made from various materials, often clay or a translucent stone called *alabaster,* and formed into various shapes. They could be decorated elaborately or simply, as long as they represented these four traditional figures: falcon, baboon, jackal, and man. For your jars, collect four used brown cardboard tubs from an ice cream shop to use as a base. On the lid, form the head of the figure by wadding, twisting, and crumpling

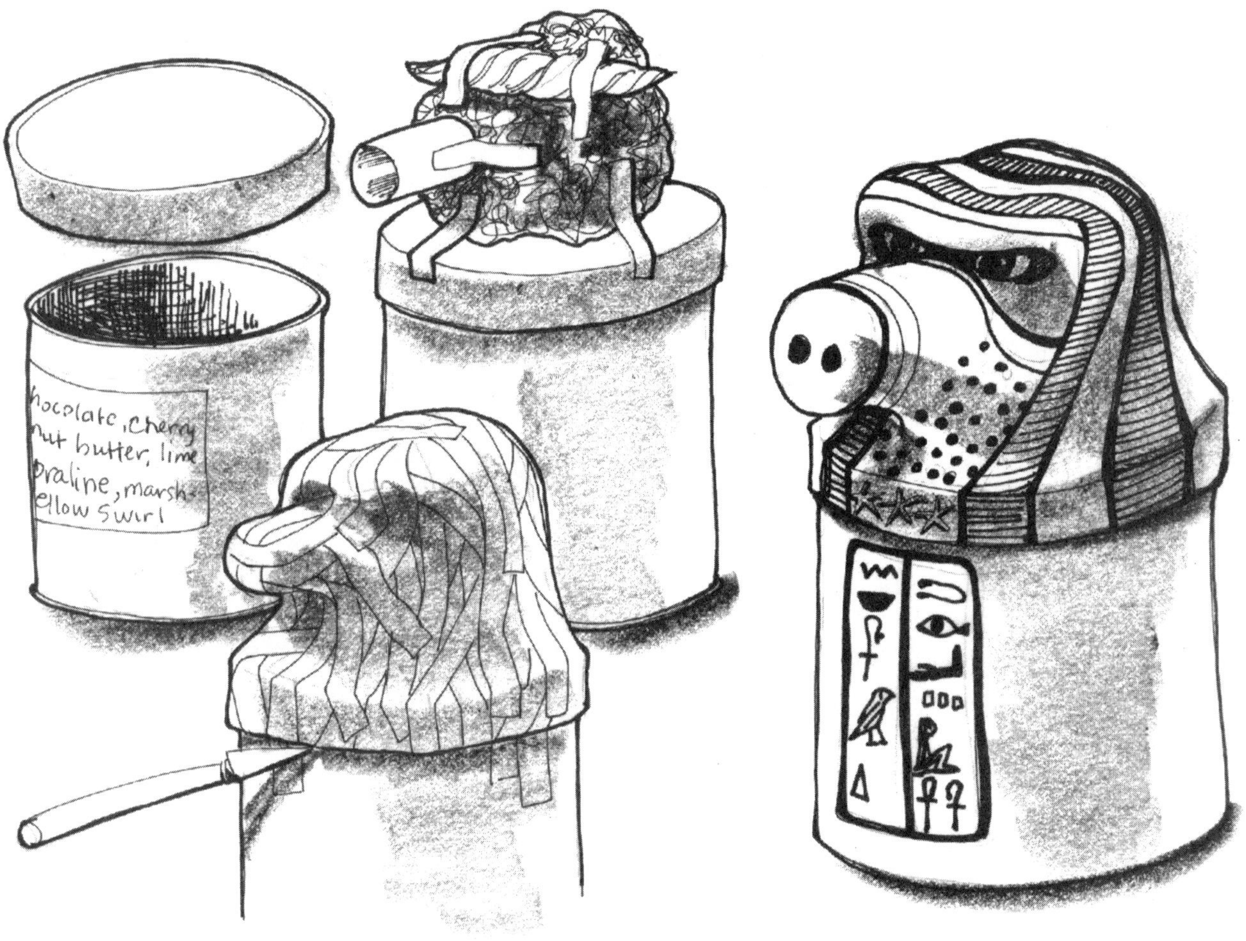
hocolate, cherry
nut butter, lime
praline, marsh-
ellow Swirl

newspaper into the desired shape. Secure it in place with a little masking tape as shown above. You may also use cardboard tubes or chunks of plastic foam in the process which can be taped in the same manner as the newspaper. Apply several layers of newspaper that has been torn into 1" strips, dipped into wallpaper paste (prepared as package instructions advise), and then pulled gently between the fingers to remove excess paste. Work with the lid in place on the tub as otherwise it may warp in the drying process. Strips that extend onto the tub itself can be trimmed later. When the lid has achieved the desired shape, apply a final layer of paper towels. This creates a smooth surface that is easy to mark. Allow to dry completely. Cut the lid from the tub and tape any rough edges with masking tape. Designate areas to be painted with pencil or marker. Then apply tempera or acrylic paint to complete the jars. Add a few hieroglyphics to the front of the jars as cryptic labels. It is not recommended, however, that they be used for their original purpose!

Golden Coffin and Sarcophagi

Once the mummy was properly prepared and wrapped in linens, it was placed in a mummy case, usually shaped like a body, and called a *coffin* or *sarcophagus*. The inside was often painted with figures of gods of the underworld who may be helpful to the deceased on his or her journey through that place. The outside was richly decorated. The face of the coffin was an idealized portrait— how the dead person would like to appear in the afterlife. The body portion may have gods or goddesses, falcons, solar discs, lotus symbols, and spells and incantations written in hieroglyphics. Some coffins were wooden, painted, or gilded, or as King Tut's, made of pure gold and encrusted with precious and semiprecious stones. During the funeral, there was an important mouth-opening ceremony for the mummy. Special tools were used for this purpose to ensure that the dead would be able to eat, drink, and walk around during the afterlife. The family gathered to recite chants, burn incense, and grieve. If the deceased enjoyed wealth and high status, professional mourners were hired to wail and cry, wave their arms about, and throw dust on their heads.

Activities and Projects

Reproduce King Tut's coffin. Study the mummy case illustrated on page 18 and others from your research. Line up two or three identical, rectangular cardboard boxes with lids in the size you want your finished coffin. Shoeboxes would make a small coffin, a processed cheese box would make an even smaller one. Larger boxes such as those that hold folders or typing paper could be combined to make a coffin large enough for King Tut himself! Open one end of each box and lid, overlap them and tape them together as shown on page 20. Using the same method as used for the canopic jars, build up the lid to form a "human" shape. Wad up newspapers, use

heavy cardboard cut to desired shape, add cardboard tubes, plastic foam chunks, cartons, or any other lightweight material to build up the surface. Use only enough masking tape to hold pieces in place until you can cover them with newspaper strips dipped in wallpaper paste.

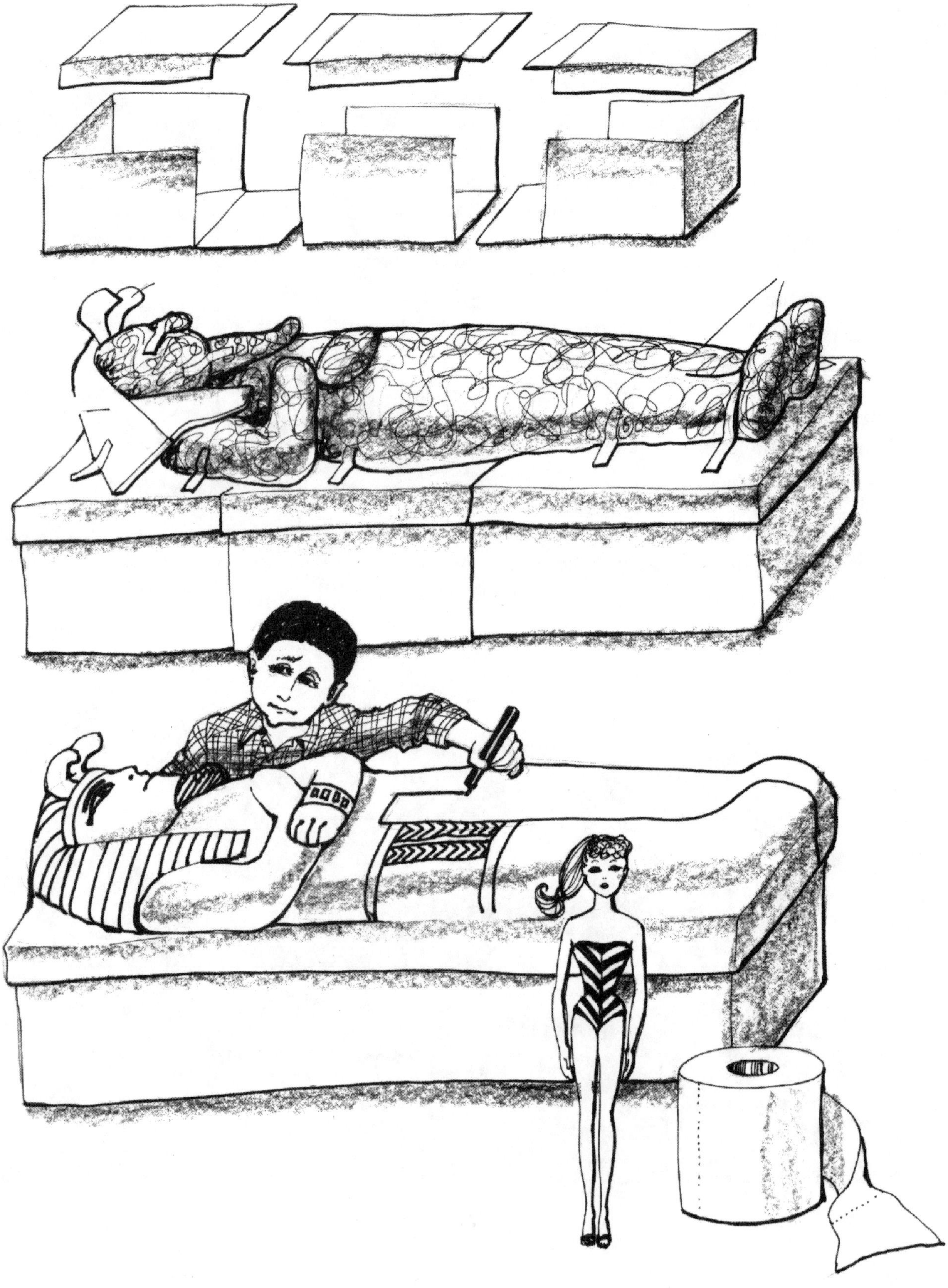

Add a final layer of brown paper towels on top. Allow the coffin to dry completely with the lid in place on the top to prevent warping. Outside, spray the entire coffin with quick-dry gold spray paint. Then carefully mark the areas to be decorated Egyptian-style. Paint with tempera or more permanent acrylic. What coffin would be complete without a mummy inside? Borrow a doll to fit your coffin, or roll and fold newspapers into a body shape. If you are making a life-size coffin, stuff an old, long-sleeved shirt and pants with newspaper and use a ball for the head. Wrap the figure with toilet paper or white cotton strips of old sheeting and place it in your coffin. This project doubles as a Halloween prop for the local haunted house!

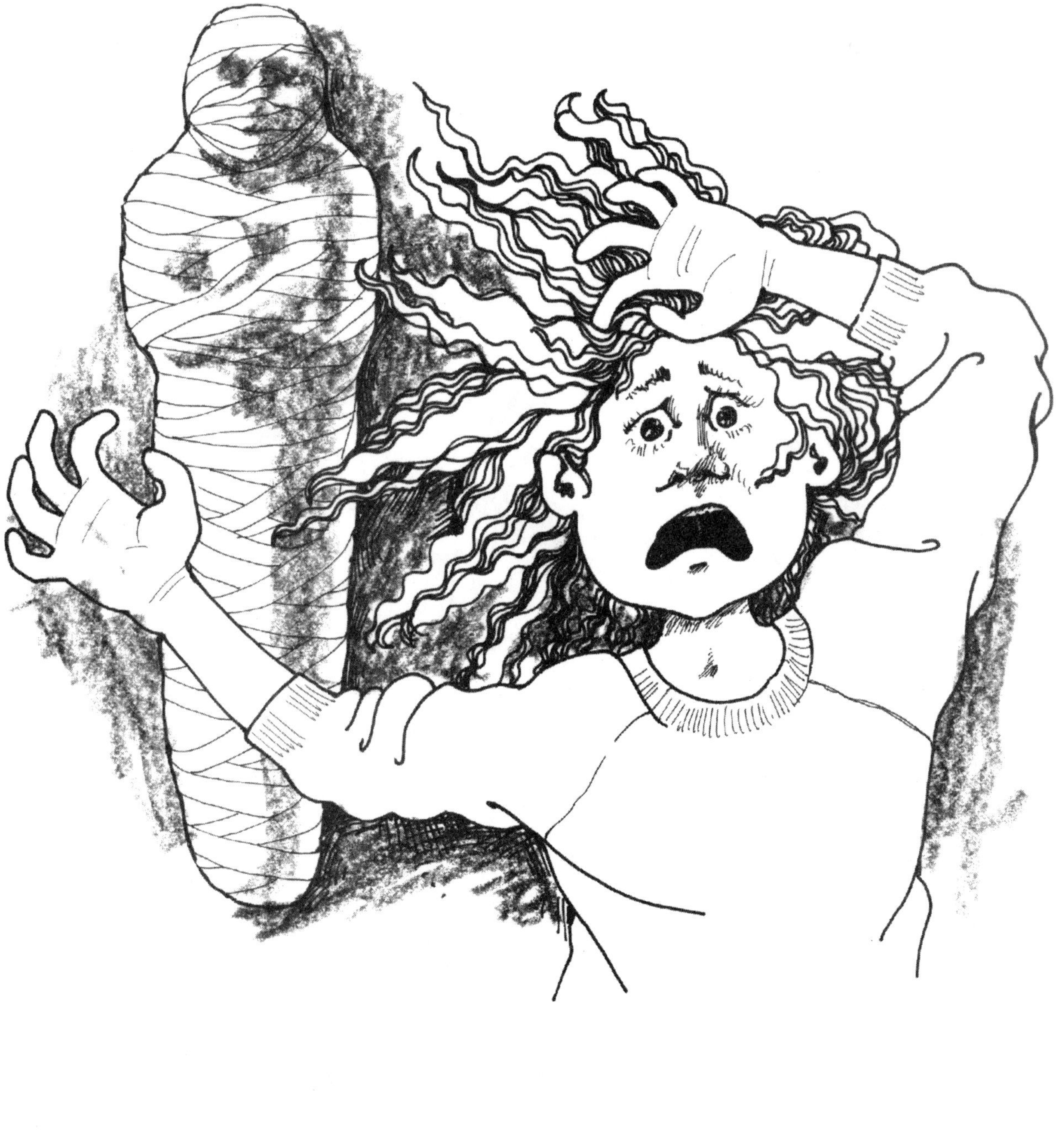

Inside the Tomb

Once the mummy was safely inside the coffin, it was often placed inside a modest monument—a pile of stones the size of a mountain—a pyramid. Deep in the heart of the pyramid lay the burial chamber, reachable only by narrow, secret passageways created to discourage grave-robbers. Since the tomb was also filled with everything the deceased could possibly need to thoroughly enjoy the afterlife, there was plenty to rob. Those tombs that have been discovered intact tell us about almost every aspect of life in ancient Egypt. The walls are painted with murals depicting Egyptian gods and goddesses such as Osiris, god of the underworld; Isis, his wife; Thoth, the ibis-headed god of wisdom; Horus, the falcon-headed sky god; Anubis, the jackal-headed god of mummification; and Amon-Re, the sun god. Each of these gods took part in the death process of the deceased.

Horus   Thoth   Anubis

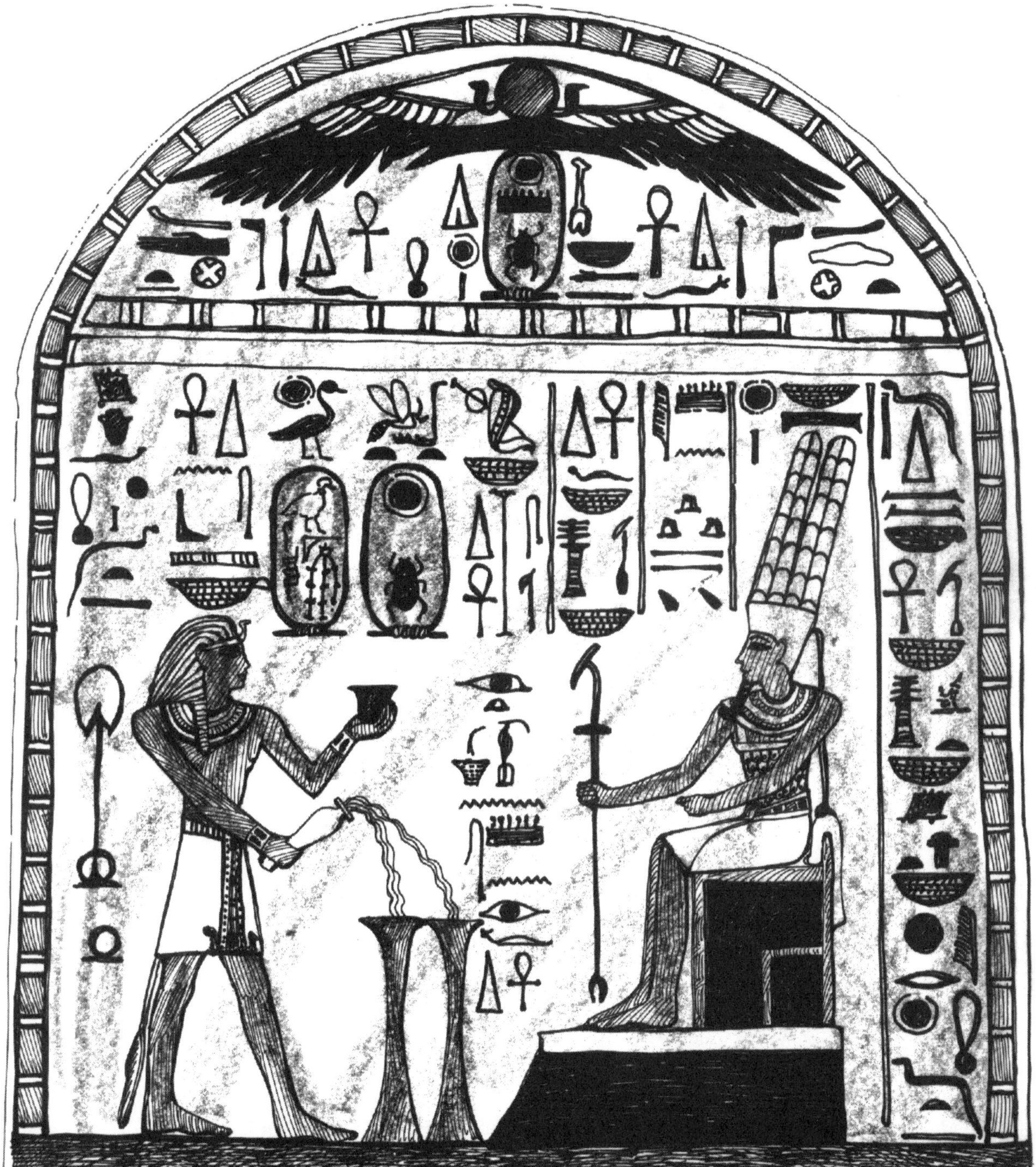

Picking
Grapes

Spiritual subjects are not the only ones painted on the walls of the tombs. Farmers working the fertile soil along the Nile, fishermen, musicians, dancers, acrobats, beautiful Egyptian women applying makeup, and slaves grinding grain to make bread are all represented because it was believed that all were an important part of life beyond the grave.

The Egyptians had a unique style of painting that did not follow the rules that are followed today. They varied the size of the figures in their work according to their importance. The pharaoh would be the largest figure, and the slaves may be painted only half his size. They also showed each part of the body from its most recognizable angle; eyes and shoulders were painted from the front view while the face and lower body, legs and feet were painted from the side. This accounts for the stiff, fragmented appearance that we recognize as typically Egyptian.

Activities and Projects

Paint an Egyptian mural. Study the mural shown above and look for other examples in books from the library. Notice the general color schemes used on the murals—white, black, blue, turquoise, red, orange, gold, brown, and rusty terra cotta. Pay attention to the detail on the garments such as the jeweled collars, elaborate hairdos, and the decorative detail surrounding the figures. Be certain to investigate and identify the action taking place. Knowing what was painted and why sheds great light on the daily life in Egypt and what was considered important enough to portray. Make a thumbnail sketch (small scale) of an Egyptian scene based on your research and decide on the finished size of your work. You may choose to

work in tempera on a sheet of heavy paper, on a portion of a large roll of paper that has been affixed to the wall, or use acrylic or oils to make a permanent addition to one of the walls in your school. Working on a large scale would make a great class project. Each student could be responsible for one Egyptian figure, then all could be combined in the final piece. Transfer your thumbnail sketch to the large paper or wall using a grid system. In this system a small drawing is divided into small squares, and then the wall is divided into the same number of squares but much bigger, as shown above. Each square portion of the small drawing is then redrawn in the corresponding large square on the wall. Another method of enlarging the sketch is to use a copy machine to produce an acetate copy. Place the copy on an overhead projector, moving it forward or back until the image projected on the wall is the desired size. Trace the image all at one time because it is difficult to realign if the projector is moved. Now it's time to paint! When the work is finished, share it with others. Explain why you chose to depict what you did, and describe the important symbols contained in your work.

An alternative project is to paint a modern subject in the Egyptian style. Choose an everyday activity that you enjoy such as playing sports or video games, eating at a fast-food restaurant, or even walking down the halls of the school. Design a mural depicting this scene, only follow the Egyptian rules of figure drawing. Think of what students will learn from such a mural 4,000 years in the future.

Amulets

The Egyptian pharaohs relied on the gods and goddesses in the temples for help and guidance, but ordinary Egyptians had little access to them. They relied instead on medicinal plants, magic spells, and amulets. Amulets were worn as pendants on necklaces, belts, and bracelets for protection while a person lived. When a person died, amulets were also enclosed in the linen wrappings of the mummy for extra protection. They were made from

almost anything—gold, electrum (mixture of gold and silver), jewels, stones, or clay. Children sometimes wore fish amulets in their hair to prevent drowning in the Nile. The scarab beetle symbolized the sun god when he took the form of Khepri at dawn and pushed the sun across the sky just as the real beetle pushes a ball of dung around. It sometimes appears winged. The ibis amulet represents Thoth, god of wisdom and

Scarab

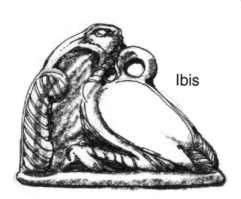

Ibis

writing. The eye (shown at left) can represent both the vengeful form of the sun god, and Horus, the falcon-headed god of the sky. It was thought to protect everything behind it. Eyes like these were formed of wax and used to plug holes cut in the body during the mummification process. Necklaces of silver and other metals in the form of an eye wore worn even by Bastet, the cat goddess, and an eye was sometimes tattooed directly onto the chest for everlasting protection. The pillar of Osiris was worn in honor of Osiris, the god of afterlife. The goddess of millions of years, Heh, was worn to ensure a long life, and cowrie shells were worn by women who hoped for many children. Clearly, these people took no chances. Sometimes the amulet and small pieces of papyrus with protective spells written on them were placed in a case and worn around the neck.

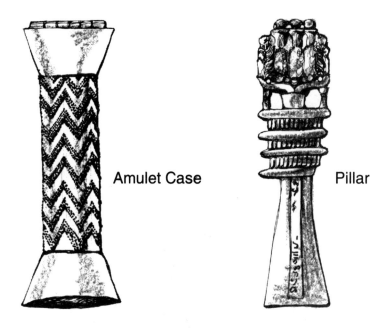

Amulet Case

Pillar

Activities and Projects

Protect yourself with an amulet. Study the examples of amulets illustrated on pages 26 through 28. Then design one of your own according to your needs. Use a small knife to carefully cut an outline shape of your design from small pieces of heavy cardboard such as mat board or the backing of pads of paper. (Framing shops will sometimes give away their scraps.) Cut smaller pieces and use white glue to glue them to the outline shape to build up the figure and create three-dimensionality. Add details by gluing on bits and pieces of twisted aluminum foil, dried beans, rice, macaroni, wire, beads, or plastic. Add a small loop or bore a hole through the top of the cardboard for hanging. When the amulet has dried completely, apply several light coats of metallic gold spray paint to the front and the back until the piece is completely covered. When this process is complete, glue on "jewels" of colored plastic, beads, or glass. Make your amulet into a necklace or bracelet by stringing it along with some beads onto embroidery floss or strong thread. Be sure to leave enough length on the string to tie a knot.

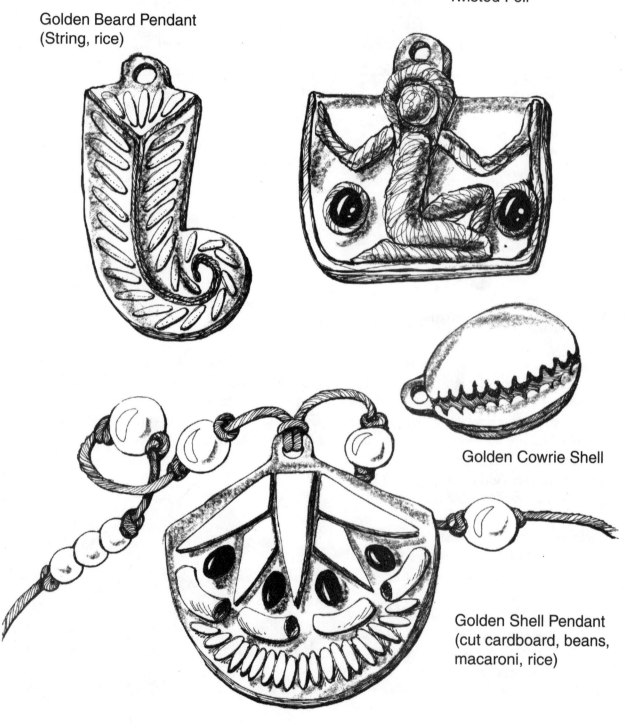

Golden Beard Pendant
(String, rice)

Twisted Foil

Golden Cowrie Shell

Golden Shell Pendant
(cut cardboard, beans,
macaroni, rice)

Ancient Greek Art

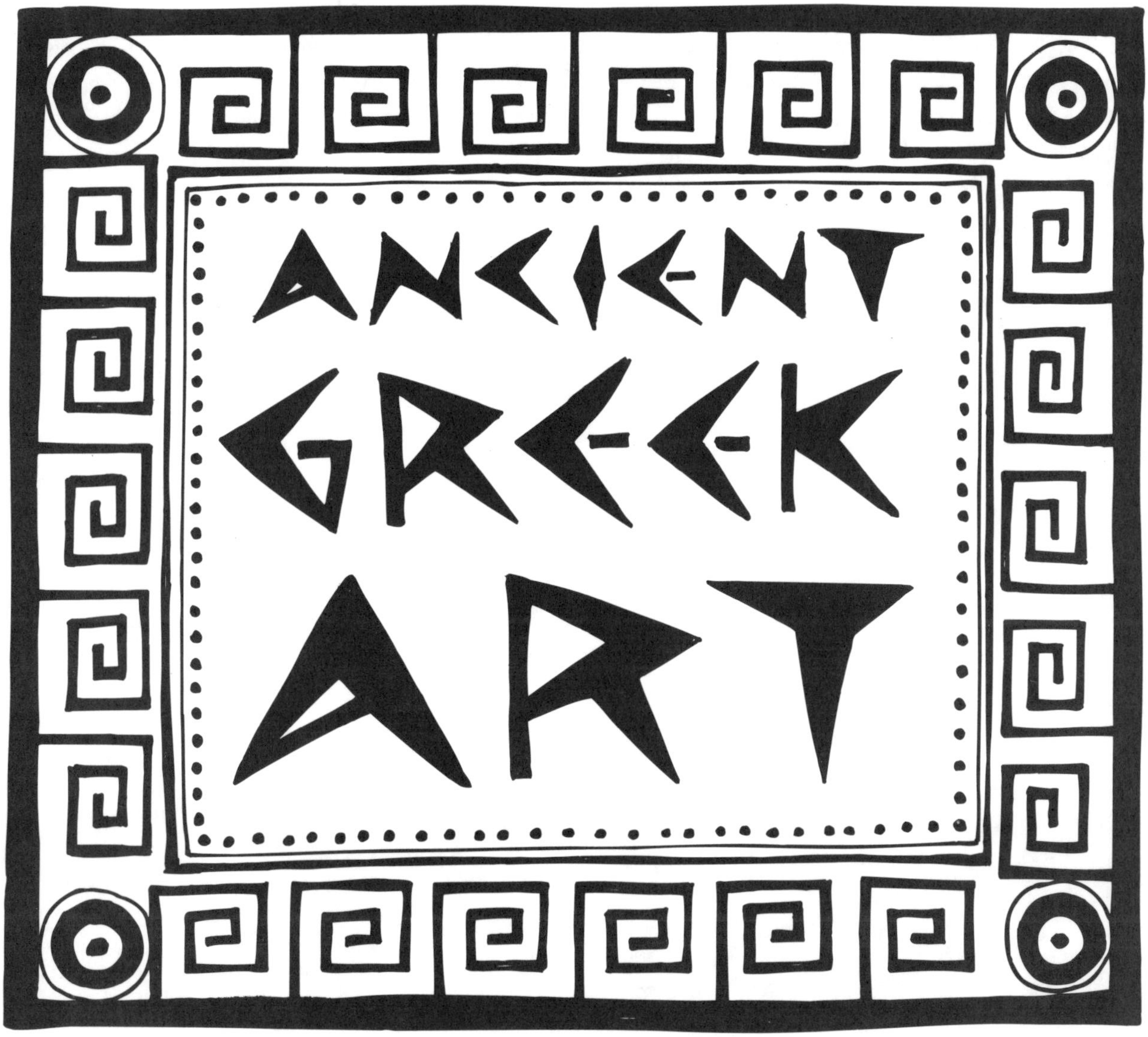
ANCIENT
GREEK
ART

In the thousand years or so before the birth of Christ, another great civilization was thriving just across the Mediterranean from Egypt in what is now Greece. Greece began as separate city-states, each with its own king, and often warring among themselves. Sparta was fierce and warlike, while Athens' strength was her wisdom. Knossos, ruled by King Minos, on the island of Crete was one of the first city-states, and legend has it that there was a ferocious bull-headed monster, the Minotaur, living in a labyrinth beneath the castle.

Though the glory of ancient Greece no longer exists, her legacy has been passed on to the western world through art, drama, philosophy, and even the Olympic games. But most important perhaps is the idea that humans should be allowed to govern themselves—an idea known today as democracy.

Mosaics and the *Odyssey*

Mosaic is an art form that has been used by many different cultures throughout the centuries. Floor mosaics appeared in ancient Greece in the fourth century B.C. At this time, water-rounded pebbles of different colors were set close together in a cement-like base. About a century later, tiny, flat pieces of colorful stones replaced the pebbles so that the floors were smoother. The small stone pieces were placed in such a way so as to create designs and scenes of hunts, battles, everyday life, or legends.

One legend that was popular among the Greeks was the *Odyssey*. This epic poem was written by a Greek poet named Homer who, according to tradition, was blind. The story is about Odysseus, the king of Ithaca, a Greek Island, and his adventures as he tries to return home after the Trojan War. The journey took Odysseus ten years to complete. Along the way he encountered storms, sea nymphs, lotus-eaters, a Cyclops, and much more.

Activities and Projects

Create a mosaic using a Greek legend as the subject matter. Study Homer's *Odyssey* (in an abridged, illustrated form) and make a small sketch of your favorite part. Be sure to keep the lines in the drawing very simple because small details are difficult to show successfully in mosaics. When you are satisfied with your design, go over the lines with a felt-tip pen and enlarge it on a copy machine to the size of the finished piece or use the grid system. Transfer this design onto a backing of stiff cardboard, mat board, foam core

board, masonite, paneling, or other stiff surface that has been cut three inches larger in length and width than the size of the design. Leave a margin of one and one-half inches around the design while transferring it. Ask a tile store for sample chips of countertop material. These usually come on a little chain in many colors. If these are unavailable, any colored paper that can be cut into pieces will work—wallpaper, mat paper, giftwrapping paper, construction paper. The chips are preferable because they are permanent and will not fade. Plan the colors of the mosaic carefully, choosing contrasting colors for objects adjacent to one another so they will show up well.

The sample tile chips can be easily broken into pieces measuring ½" x ½" or smaller using a pair of glazier's pliers. Hold the tile upside-down against the table and gently snap upwards as shown below. Place tiles of each color range needed in plastic containers with lids (such as

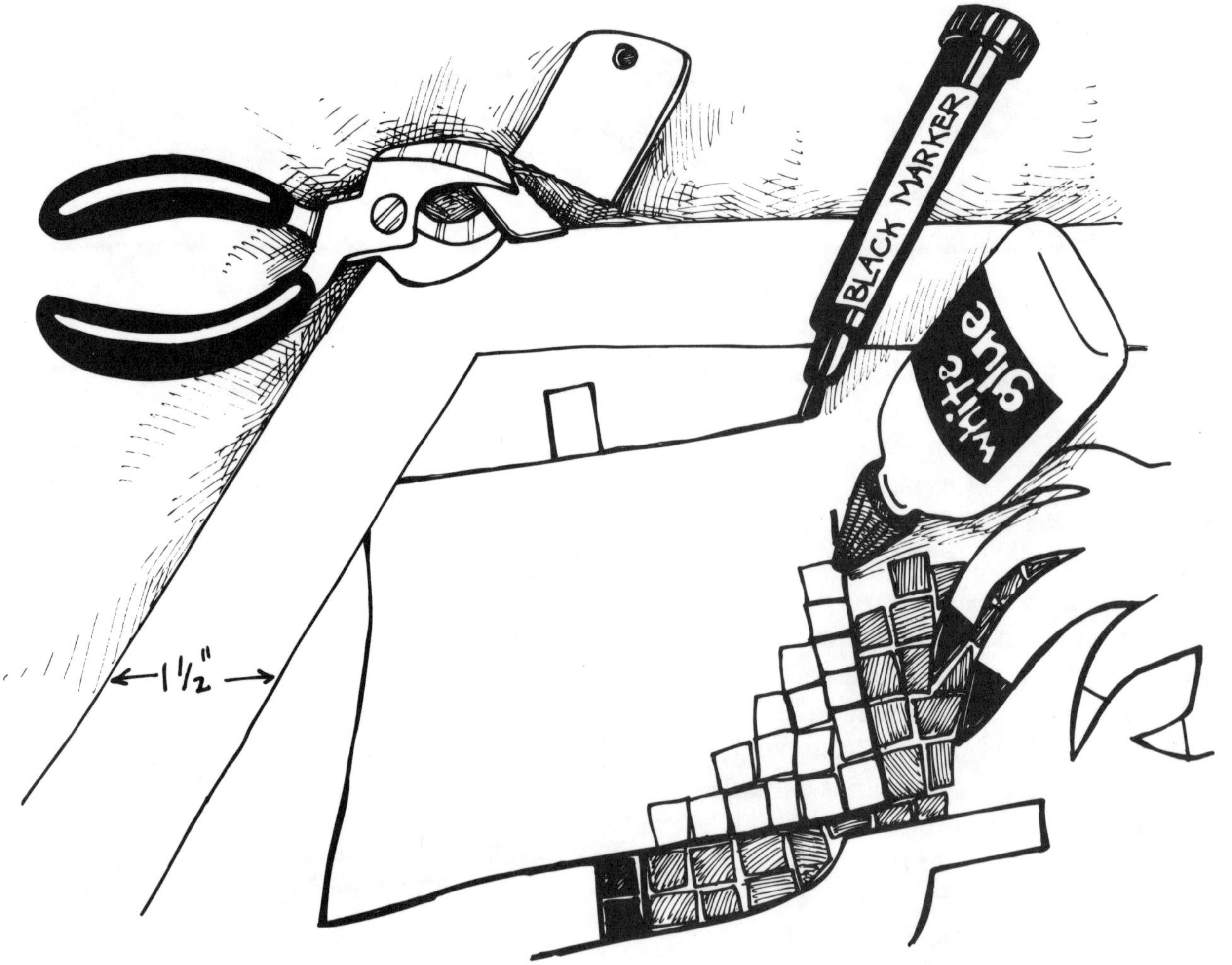
BLACK MARKER
white glue
1½"

margarine tubs) until they are needed so they do not become mixed-up. Glue the tiles onto the backing with white glue or wood glue. This adheres well because the back of the tiles is rough. Glue tiles around the outline of each object first, placing the outside edge of each tile along the edge. Then fill in the inside keeping tiles as close together as possible. Keep the pliers handy in case you need to nip the edges to reshape a tile so it fits perfectly.

Finish the mosaic by gluing one and one-half-inch strips of wooden lath or crescent mat board around the edge margins. Mat board can be cut easily on a paper cutter.

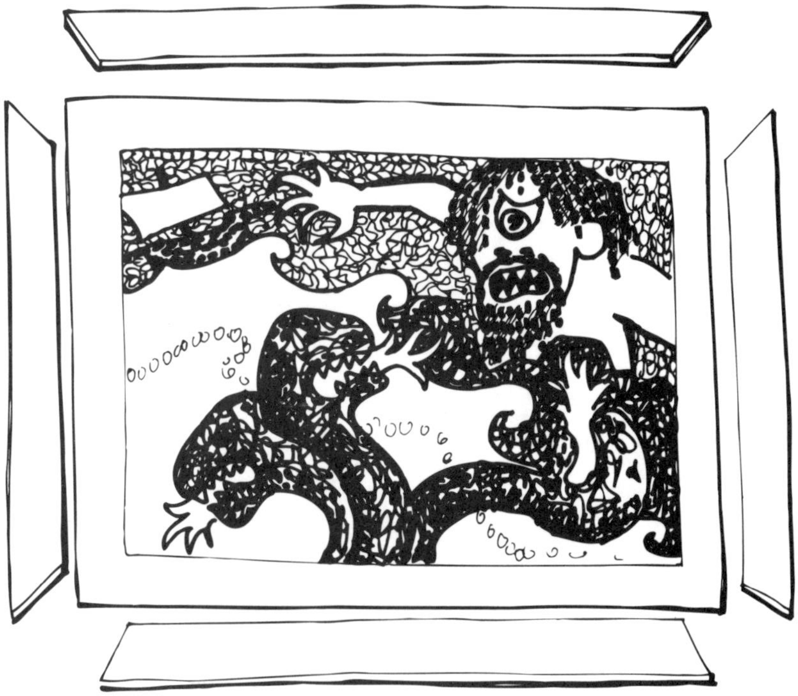

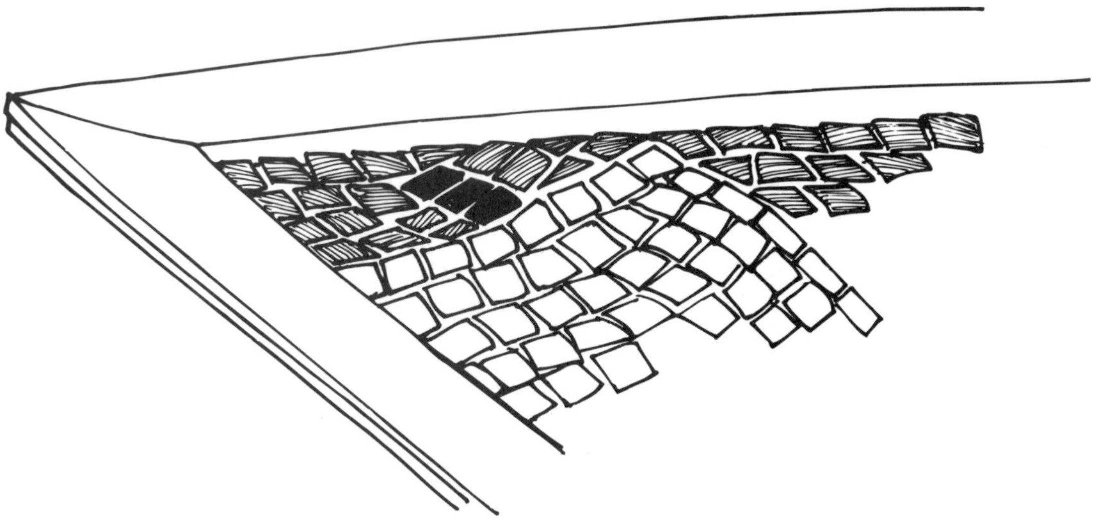

Greek Gods and the Parthenon

The Greeks of ancient times believed that twelve gods and goddesses, who were immortal, sat on thrones of gold atop Mount Olympus and ruled the lives of the mortals below. Those twelve were

Zeus—the mightiest, ruler of all divinities; his sacred animal was the bull.

Hera—sister and wife of Zeus, protector of marriage and women; her favorite bird was the peacock.

Apollo—god of light, poetry, music, and purity.

Artemis—Apollo's twin sister, goddess of hunting and childbirth.

Athena—goddess of wisdom, crafts, and war; she sprang fully grown from Zeus' head; her sacred animal was the heifer.

Aphrodite—goddess of love, the most beautiful of all, whose son Eros would use his golden bow and arrows to shoot unwary victims and cause them to fall in love.

Ares—vain and cruel god of war; Eris, the spirit of strife, was always with him.

Hephaestus—blacksmith for the gods and god of fire and metalworking.

Hermes—messenger for the gods; god of shepherds, travelers, merchants, thieves, and all others who lived by their wits.

Demeter—goddess of the harvest.

Poseidon—god of the sea, earthquakes, and horses.

Dionysus—god of wine and wild behavior; he replaced kind-hearted Hestia, goddess of the hearth, on the twelfth throne.

In addition to these twelve gods, there was Hades, dreaded and hated, who had his own kingdom—the Underworld. Many other lesser gods were thought to live on Earth such as Pan, god of nature, and nine daughters of Zeus, called the Muses. There were also nymphs, female spirits of nature, and heroes who were humans favored by the gods and who performed great deeds. The Greeks loved to listen to stories, or myths, about all of these characters.

Athena is the goddess after whom Athens was named. Athens partly owes its greatness to a wise statesman named Solon who introduced democracy in 594 B.C. He cancelled all debts and freed the people who were enslaved. He divided the people into classes based on their wealth and drew up a code of law.

As Athens prospered, beautiful temples including the Parthenon were built. Dedicated to Athena herself, the Parthenon rests atop a high, flat hill called the Acropolis overlooking the city. The Parthenon, made of white marble, was huge by Greek standards—110 feet wide, 237 feet long, and about 60 feet high. It has 8 columns across the front and back, and 17 down each side. Each column is made in the plainest order of Greek architecture called "Doric" style. The triangular pieces at the top of the front and back, the pediments, were once filled with statues that told the story of the birth and life of Athena. These statues were "in the round," or carved front and back, while the frieze of statues that runs around the top of the Parthenon are "in relief," which means just the front of the figures are carved into a long, solid piece.

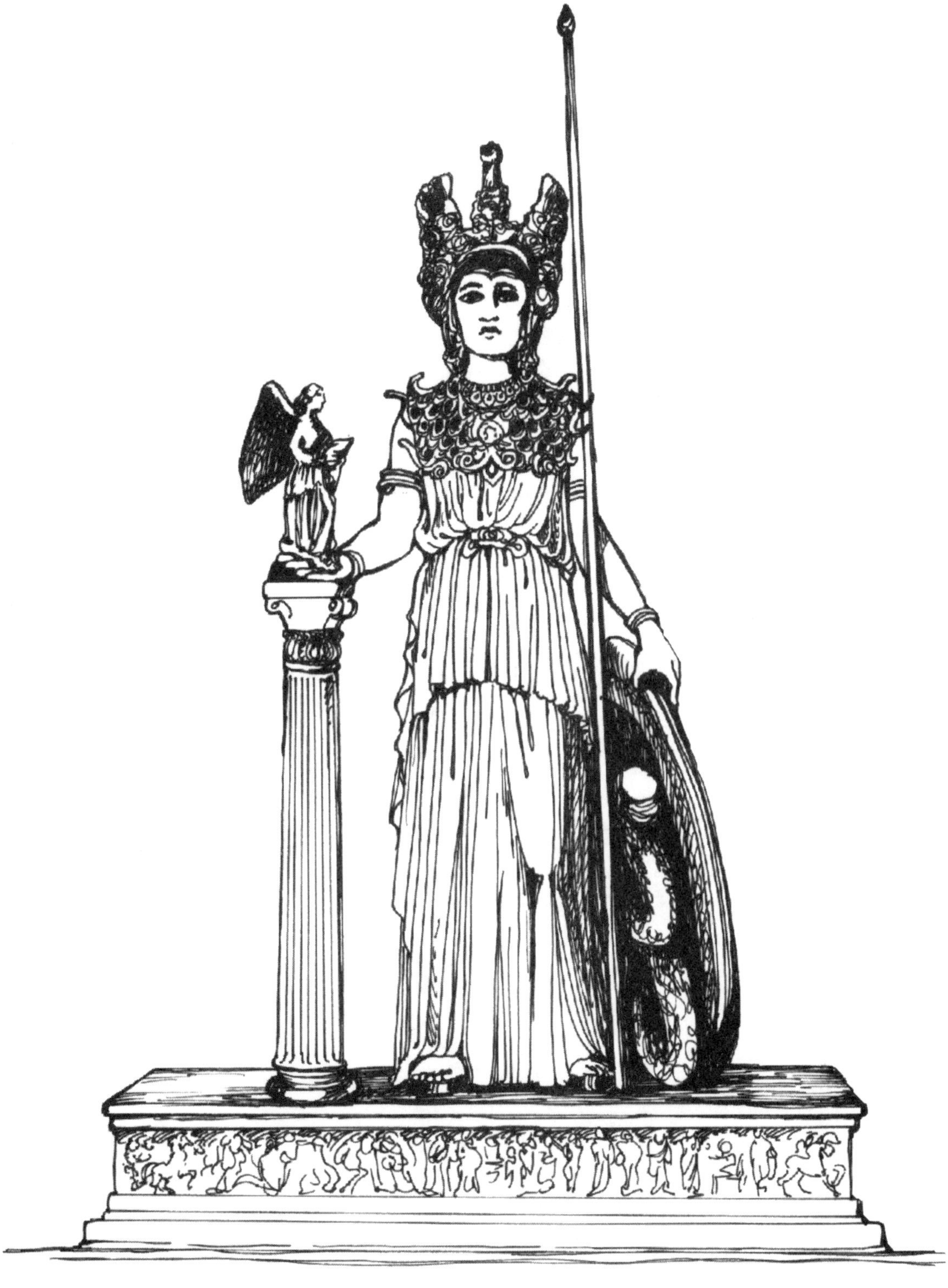

Activities and Projects

Make a paper model of Athena's temple on the Acropolis, the Parthenon. Study the pattern shown below which is drawn to scale, and enlarge it to the desired size. Use a large rectangular piece of cardboard or foam core as a base, and cut five more rectangles to fit on top of it to form the stairs around the temple. Now copy the four sides of the building onto heavy paper, as shown and cut them out using a knife. Glue on extra strips of paper to create a three-dimensional effect. Add details with pencil and colored pencil. The Greeks often painted details with reds, blues, yellows, and greens though this paint has long since worn away. Use tabs to glue the sides together and to glue them onto the base. Glue the statue of Athena onto the base. Then add the roof and the additional statues which have been drawn and cut out of heavy paper. The gold and ivory statue of Athena was created by the sculptor Phidias. Though it no longer exists, it once stood forty feet high inside the temple, with a shallow, rectangular pool in front. Use blue-green watercolor to paint the pool onto the appropriate spot on the base, and cover it with acetate or plastic wrap so that it appears wet. Add a few dark green pointed trees along the side of the temple for a finishing touch.

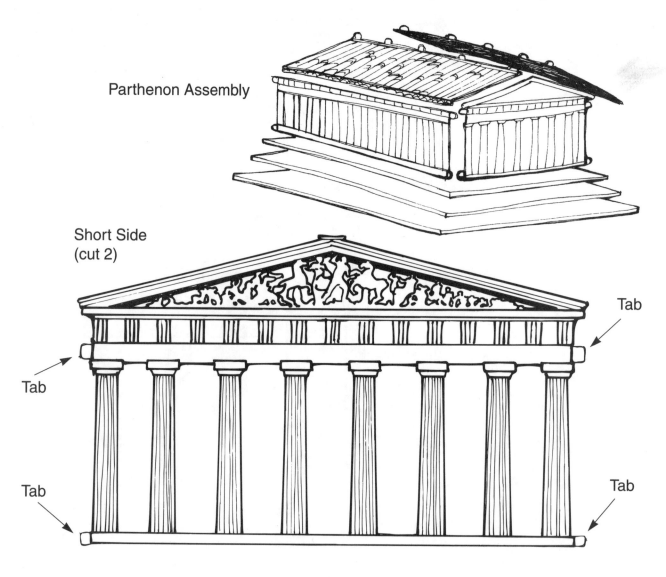

Parthenon Assembly

Short Side
(cut 2)

Tab

Tab

Tab

Tab

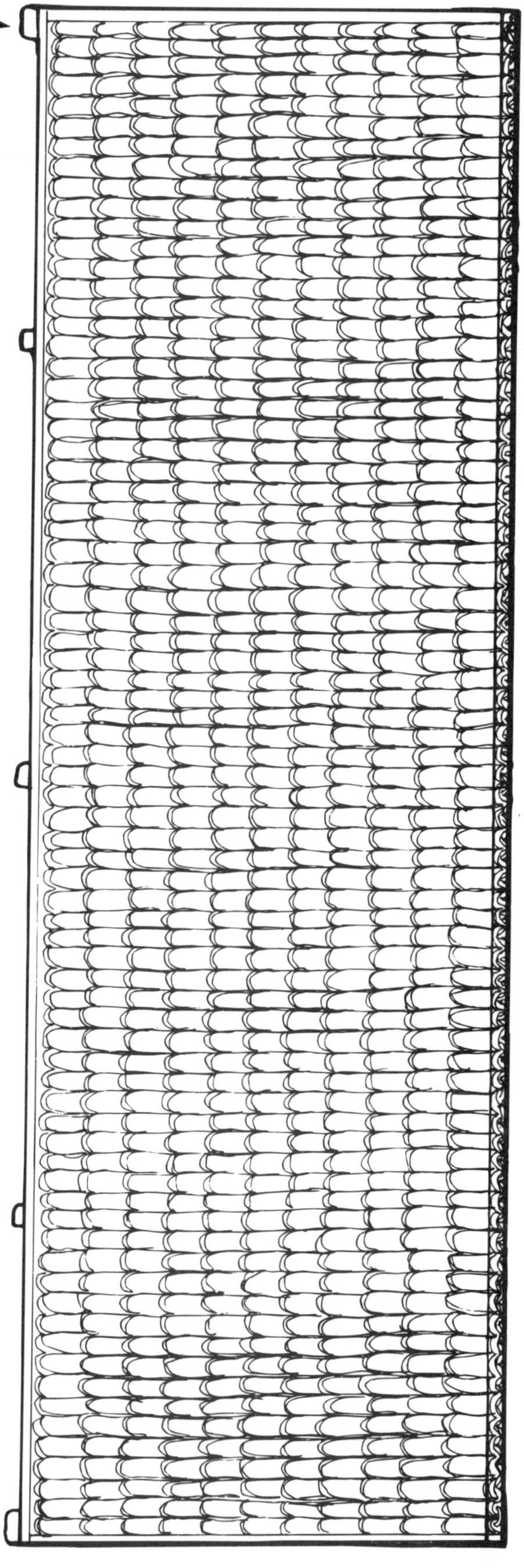
Roof
(cut 2)

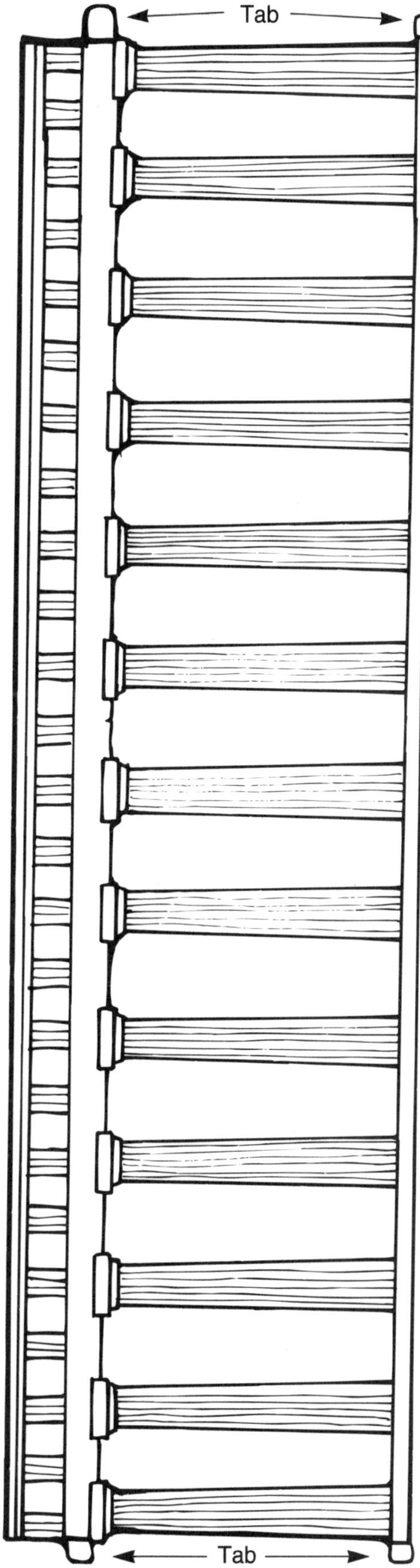
Tab
Long Side
(cut 2)
Tab

Sophocles, the Theater, and Masks

On the south slope of the Acropolis lay the theater of Dionysus, the god of wine and wild behavior. This structure, which could hold 18,000 people, was originally built for a yearly festival to honor Dionysus. The festival included singing and dancing and celebrated a good harvest, especially of grapes. The performances evolved into a play form that we recognize today as the beginning of theater. Each day of the festival, beginning at dawn, three tragedies were performed which taught the citizens of Athens about the nature of mankind, and the problems in dealing with good and evil forces in the world.

One very famous writer of tragedy was Sophocles. He wrote the play called, "Oedipus Rex" in which it was prophesied that the baby Oedipus would kill his father. Oedipus's frightened parents instructed a slave to leave him on a mountain to die. A shepherd finds him and takes him to far away Corinth where he grows up. He learns of the prophesy one day and, afraid he will kill his adopted father who he thinks is his birth father, he runs away. On the road he argues with and kills a man and later finds out that this was his true father—the prophesy had come true after all. Oedipus, a broken man, gashes out his own eyes.

Actors performing in ancient Greece often wore oversized masks with exaggerated features. Sometimes the masks had megaphone mouths. The masks were worn by the actors so even the Athenians in the back row could hear the words and see the expressions of the faces. Masks also enabled two or three actors to play more than one part easily by quickly switching masks. The masks were made of wood, cork, thin metal, or of a kind of paper-mâché.

Activities and Projects

Make a mask for a Greek play. Study the examples shown on page 40 and then design your own for a character in your play. Though the ancient Greeks began their masks by spreading the actor's face with olive oil and then wrapping the face with linen strips, begin your mask by tightly wadding newspapers in the shape and size of a face. Secure the shape with masking tape. Cover the newspaper with foil or plastic wrap so that the finished mask can be removed from this armature. Mix wallpaper paste according to the directions on the package. Dip torn newspaper strips about one and one-half inches wide into the paste, and then pull the strips gently between your fingers to remove excess paste. Apply several layers of these strips over the mask shape horizontally and vertically. Crumple and twist more newspaper into various shapes and attach them with additional pasted strips to build up brows, noses, and other exaggerated facial features. When the mask has achieved the desired shape, apply a final layer of paper toweling and allow it to dry completely. Carefully pull out the wad of newspaper and use a knife or scissors to trim around the edges of the mask and to cut out the mouth area and the eyes.

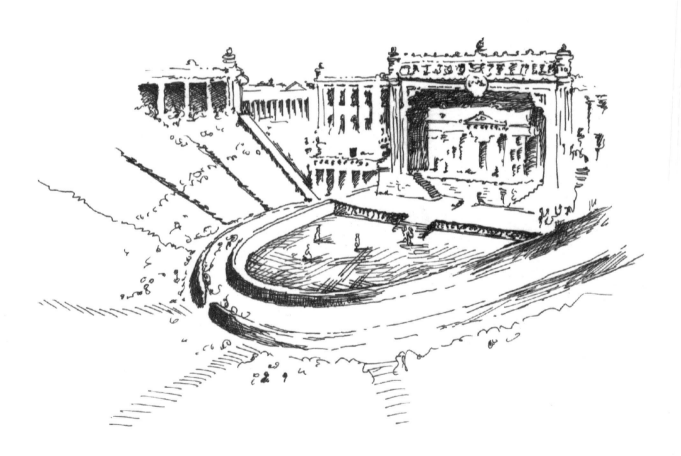

Paint the mask with tempera or acrylic paint. Make sure lips and other features are larger than life, as theatrical make-up would be. Glue or hot glue details such as hair and hair adornments, eyebrows, moustache, or beard to your mask. Get together with some friends to write and perform a tragedy.

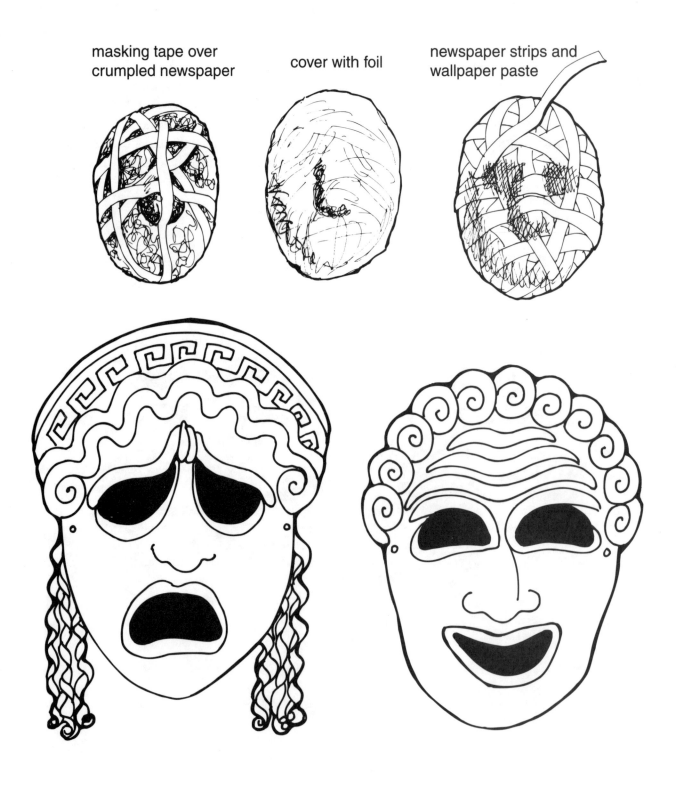

masking tape over crumpled newspaper

cover with foil

newspaper strips and wallpaper paste

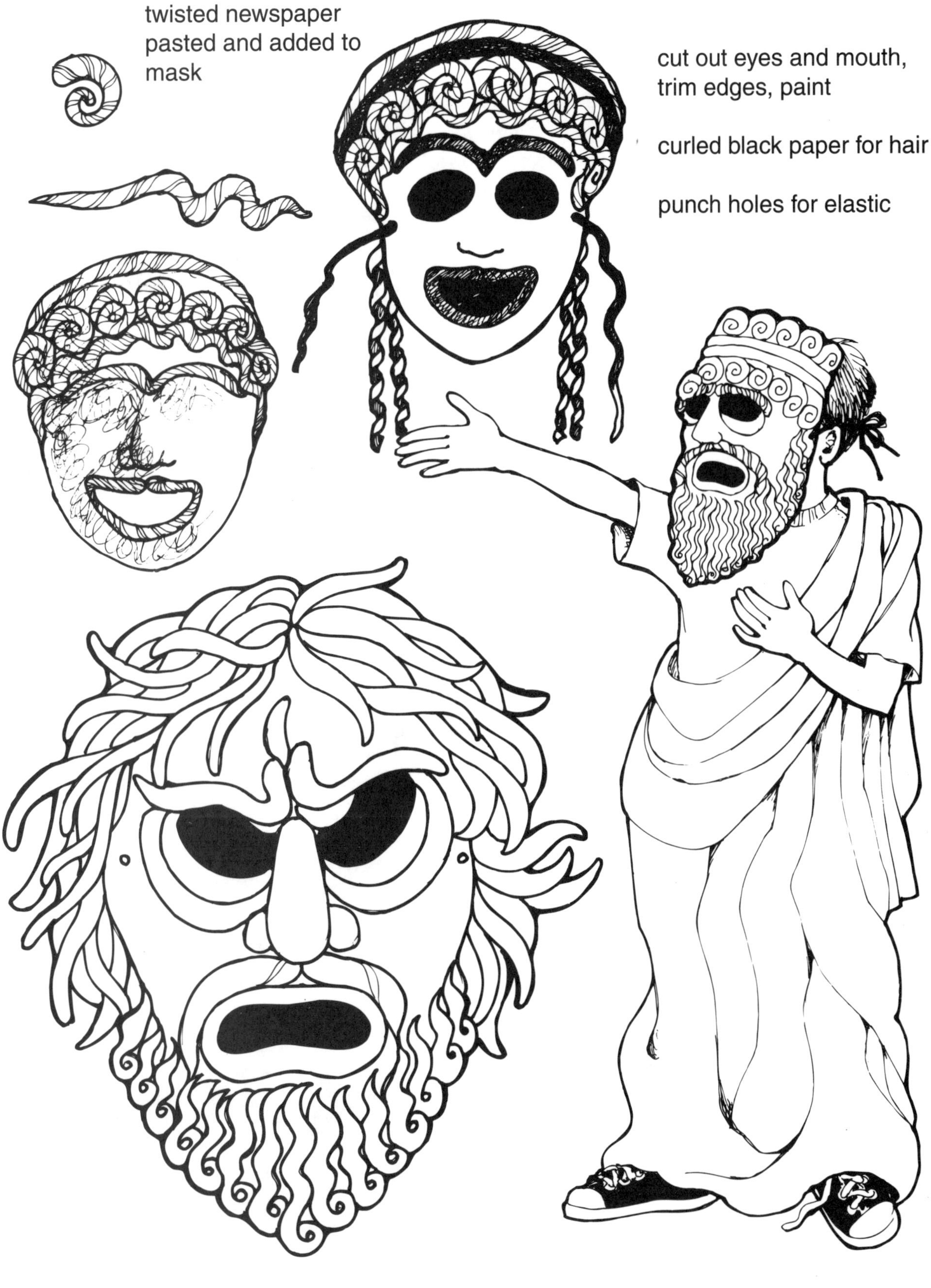
twisted newspaper
pasted and added to
mask
cut out eyes and mouth,
trim edges, paint
curled black paper for hair
punch holes for elastic

Grecian Urns

Though pottery was not the only important art form in ancient Greece, it is the one that has lasted over the years thus enabling us to study it. Around 600 B.C., the black figure technique in making pottery was popular. Silhouetted figures were painted in black onto the unfired red terra cotta pot. Details were then added by incising or scratching them on the figures. The red figure technique is exactly the opposite of the black figure technique. The red figure technique involves painting the background in black onto the pot, leaving the figures the red terra cotta color of the pot itself. Details are painted on with small brushes. This allowed the artist to show unusual views of the body with more subtle movements and twists.

The figures painted on the ancient Greek urns often depicted Greek gods and heroes from the stories the people knew and loved, but they also showed scenes from everyday life. These scenes tell us about their clothing, tools, and activities such as hunting, fishing, or spinning.

Activities and Projects

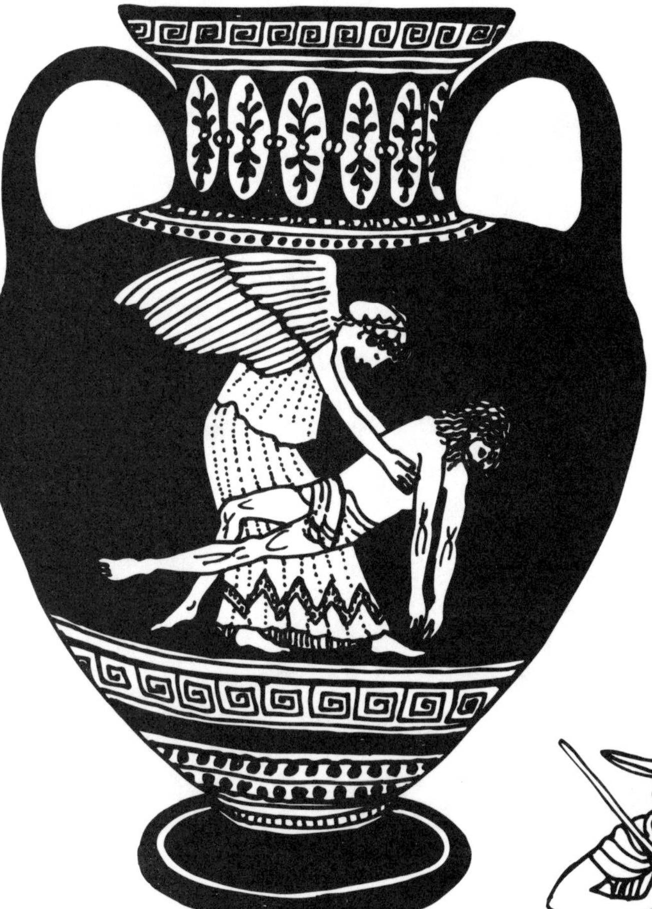

Make a Greek picture using the black or red figure technique. Study the examples shown here or others you find in the library. Sketch a figure of your own in the Greek style. Be sure to include an appropriate border design. Cut a piece of mat board, crescent board, or other stiff cardboard such as the backing of a pad of paper the same size as your sketch. Color the entire surface with a solid layer of crayon or oil pastel in a rusty red-brown color to resemble terra cotta. Lay the sketch over the colored surface and trace the lines, pressing firmly to transfer the design onto the cardboard. Paint the areas to be black with India ink to which a few drops of liquid soap has been added.

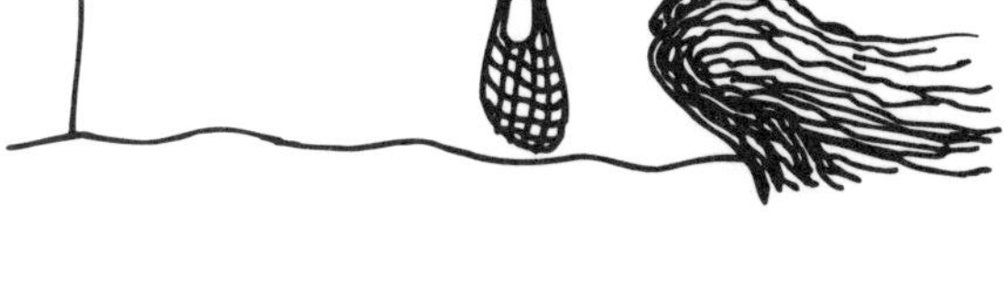

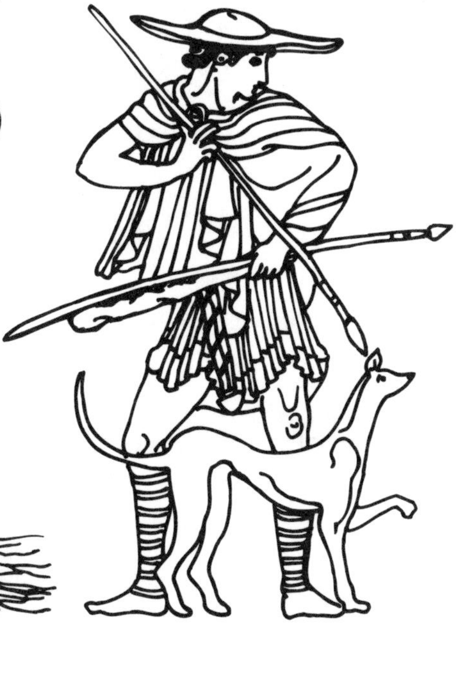

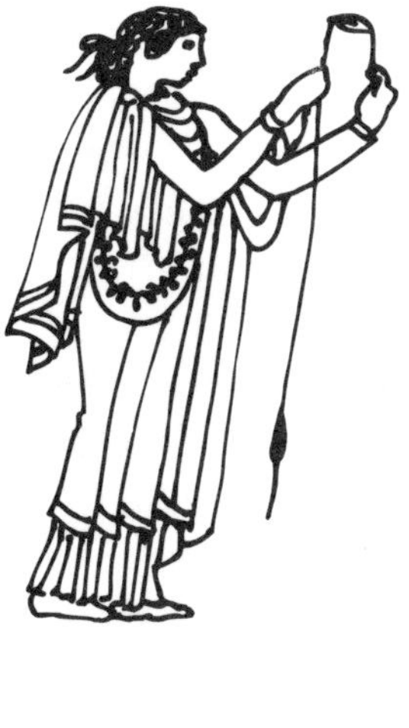

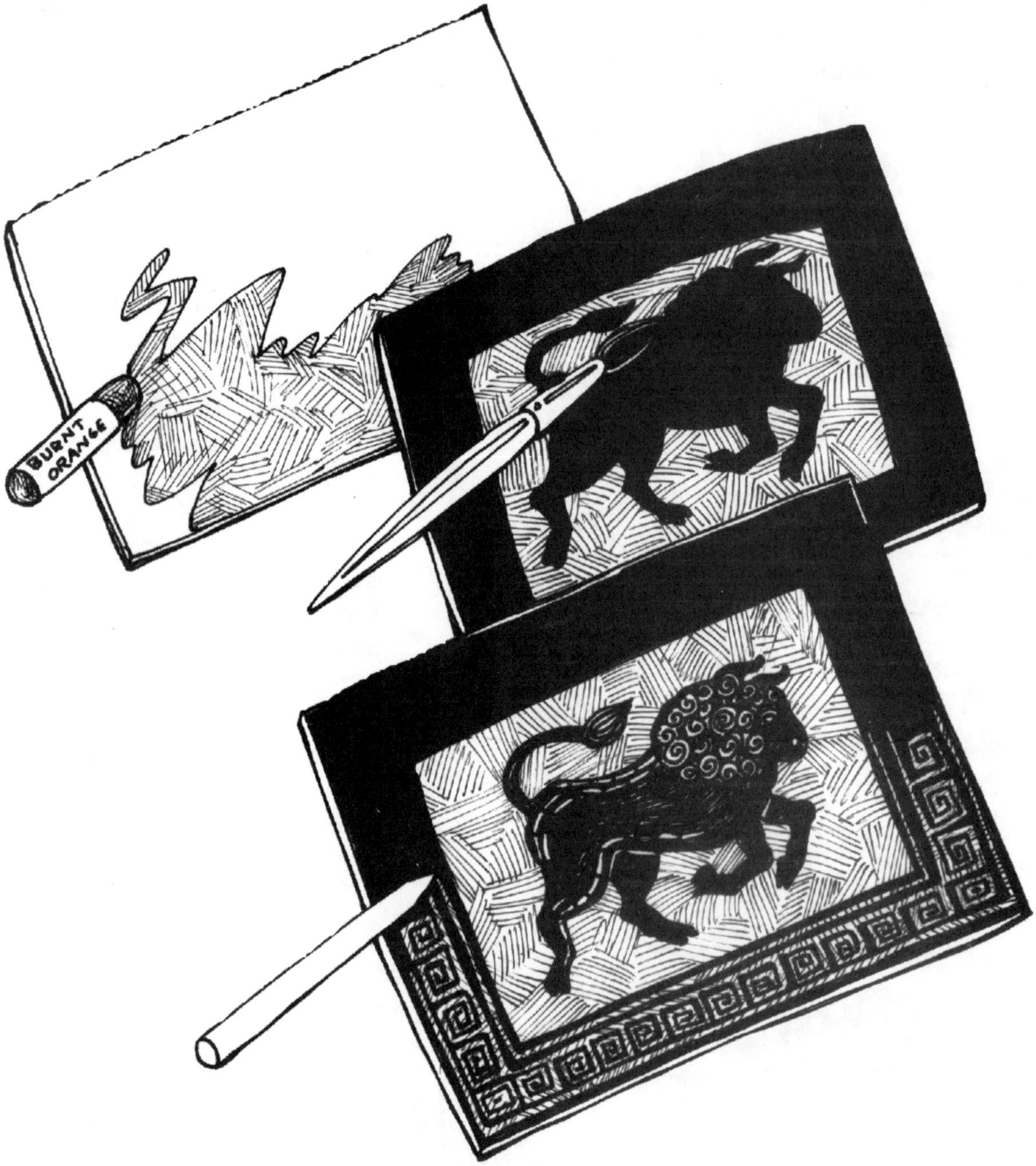
BURNT ORANGE

When the ink has dried completely, use a sharpened stick or opened paper clip to scratch the details into the black areas.

If red clay is available, use the same technique. Apply an oxide wash instead of India ink to a partially dried, but not fired, vase or tile. The piece can then be completely dried and fired in the kiln in the usual manner.

The Olympics

The very first Olympics was actually part of a religious festival with only one short footrace held in Olympia in 776 B.C. Olympia was not a town as such but, like Delphi, it was a place the Greeks went to oracles to hear prophesies about the future. The Olympics were held every four years until 394 A.D., nearly 300 times. They grew gradually larger as more events were added, until chariot races, boxing, wrestling, discus, javelin, and long jumping were all part of a huge five day festival attended by athletes from all over Greece and the Greek territories. As the competition began, the athletes stood before a forty foot statue of Zeus and vowed to play fairly. This statue was built by Phidias who also made the magnificent statue of Athena in the Parthenon in Athens. But Zeus' shrine was not the only one in Olympia. Excavations beginning in 1829 have unearthed thousands of trinkets, souvenirs, coins, and amulets made of bronze, terra cotta, and silver which athletes presented to shrines of various lesser gods in appreciation for aiding them in their victories. The winners themselves received only a headband woven of olive leaves by Olympic officials, but they were given a hero's welcome, great honor, and many gifts when they returned home.

Activities and Projects

Make a lucky object similar to one archaeologists unearthed at Olympia. Study the objects shown below and think about the kind of trinket you might use to bring you luck. Sketch your ideas on paper then use a small quantity of salt clay or cooked clay to form your trinket by pinching and shaping. Add details with sharpened sticks and other clay tools. Allow to dry completely and decide on a "faux" finish. If you want your trinket to resemble terra cotta, paint it with a rusty-red acrylic paint. Use sea-green or dark charcoal for a bronze look. When the paint is dried, add a thin watery coat of dark brown or black acrylic and wipe off the excess, or polish it with black paste shoe polish, buffing as you would leather shoes. Either of these methods will give an antiqued appearance to your trinkets. The next time you run in a race, see if your lucky trinket brings you luck!

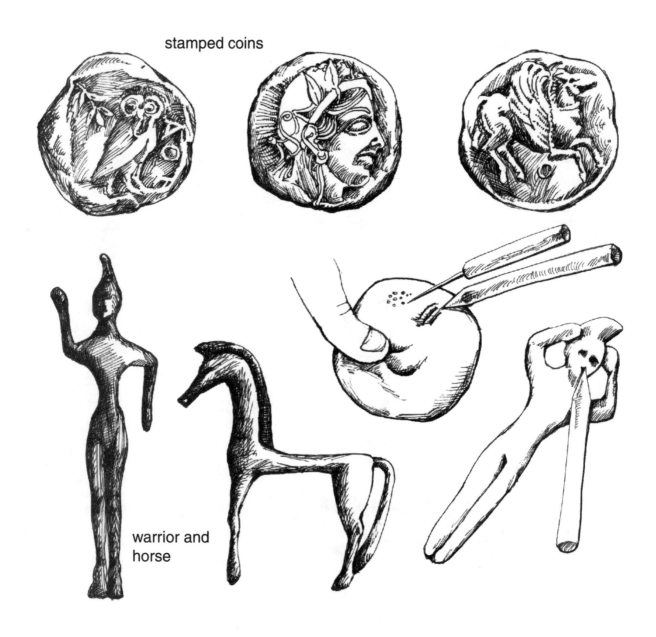

stamped coins

warrior and horse

Medieval Art

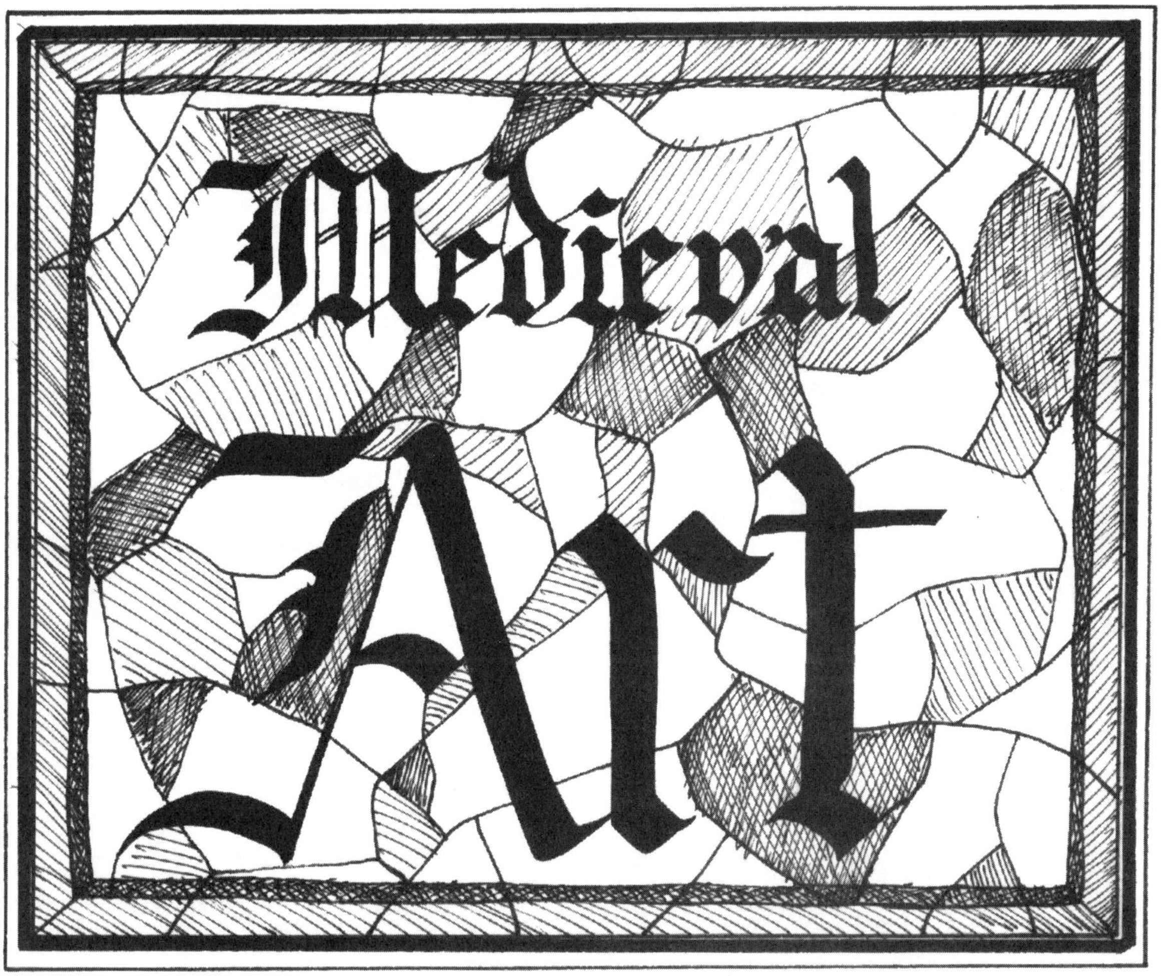
Medieval
Art

As the glory of Greece waned, the Roman Empire became the dominant power, borrowing many ideas, beliefs, and art forms from the Greeks. But beginning around 450 A.D., the Roman Empire also declined, throwing Europe into the thousand-year period we call the Middle Ages, or medieval times. Although brilliant men such as Dante wrote during this time and incredible styles of architecture such as the gothic cathedral and the castle were developed, most inhabitants of Europe during the Middle Ages were illiterate and lived in squalor in little more than hovels. There was no central government or country, and peasants obeyed the rules of the lord who lived in the manor house or castle on whose surrounding lands they lived. Rarely did they venture beyond these lands and they understood only their regional dialect and accent.

The one unifying force in this disjointed European world was the Christian church. So prevalent was Christianity that non-Christians were outcasts. When the fledgling religion of Islam grew to encompass Jerusalem, the Crusades were launched to recapture the Christian holy places there.

Tales Told on Tapestries

Cloth of the Middle Ages was made from linen, wool, or silk. Silk was a rare and very expensive luxury of the rich, imported from the Far East along dangerous trade routes. Linen was spun and woven from the fibers of the flax plant, while wool came from sheep. The animal was sheared (shaved), and the fleece (fur) was carded (combed). It was then spun into thread by spinsters and woven into cloth by websters. The fuller trampled the cloth in a trough of water which tangled the fibers and made the fabric stronger. The wet woolen cloth was stretched on a frame to dry and "teased" with the bristly head of a teasel plant to bring up loose ends which were clipped so that the fabric had a smooth finish.

Dyeing could be done before or after the wool was spun into yarn, or once the cloth was finished. People in the Middle Ages liked bright colors, so they used leaves and roots from plants to make blues, reds, and yellows. The woolen cloth was made into outer clothing such as gowns, tunics, cloaks, and leggings for men.

Wool, linen, and silk threads were also used to weave tapestries which were hung on walls and windows to keep out drafts and for decoration. Beautiful patterns of flowers and animals were designed and drawn up by a master artist and then used as a guide by the weaver who painstakingly wove each tiny detail with many different colors of thread. Tapestries were also designed to portray famous historical events such as the Bayeux Tapestry. This tapestry depicts the Norman Conquest of England in 1066 A.D., particularly the Battle of Hastings.

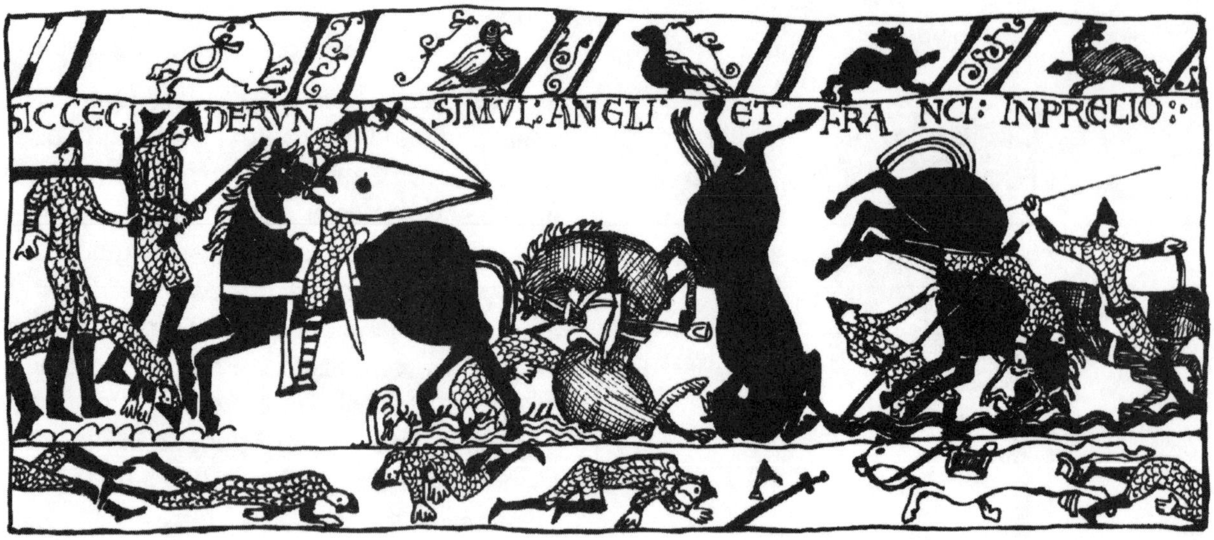
SICCECI ADERVN SIMVL: ANGLI ET FRA NCI: INPRELIO

Activities and Projects

Design and weave your own minitapestry. Sketch a very simple design of a favorite animal or flower such as the one shown on page 51. Retrace the lines with a black marker. Cut a piece of heavy cardboard or mat board one inch larger than your design. Mark and cut one-half-inch slits at one-quarter-inch intervals across the top and bottom of the mat board. Lace thin, sturdy string or yarn through the slits and around the back to form the "warp" (vertical) threads. Slide your sketch between the threads and the mat board to use as a guide while you weave your tapestry. Cut a three-foot piece of yarn of the desired color and thread it through a tapestry needle. Beginning at the bottom, weave the yarn over then under the warp across the area to be filled in. Weave it under and then over back again. When one area has been completed, go on to the next, catching the edges of the first area with the second yarn color so that the completed tapestry will hold together in one piece. Pull all the yarn ends to the back for a neat appearance. Continue until all areas have been filled in. The tapestry can be left on the mat board for display or the warp threads can be cut across the middle of the back, and tied securely to a dowel across the top and with knots across the bottom.

Using the method described above to make a tapestry with greater detail such as those that depict the story of a historic event would take a very long time, just as it did in medieval times. A shortcut is possible, however. Begin with a piece of loosely woven cloth such as burlap cut two and one-half inches larger at the top than your design. Use an indelible marker to transfer the design onto the burlap. Thread a tapestry needle with dark yarn and use an overhand stitch for the letters and to outline the objects on the tapestry. Fill in the outlined areas with yarn stitched with the satin stitch, or simply draw in stitch lines with various colors of markers. Finally, fold the top over and stitch or hot glue across it to form a tube for a dowel to slide through. Hang the tapestry in your castle.

Woven tapestry

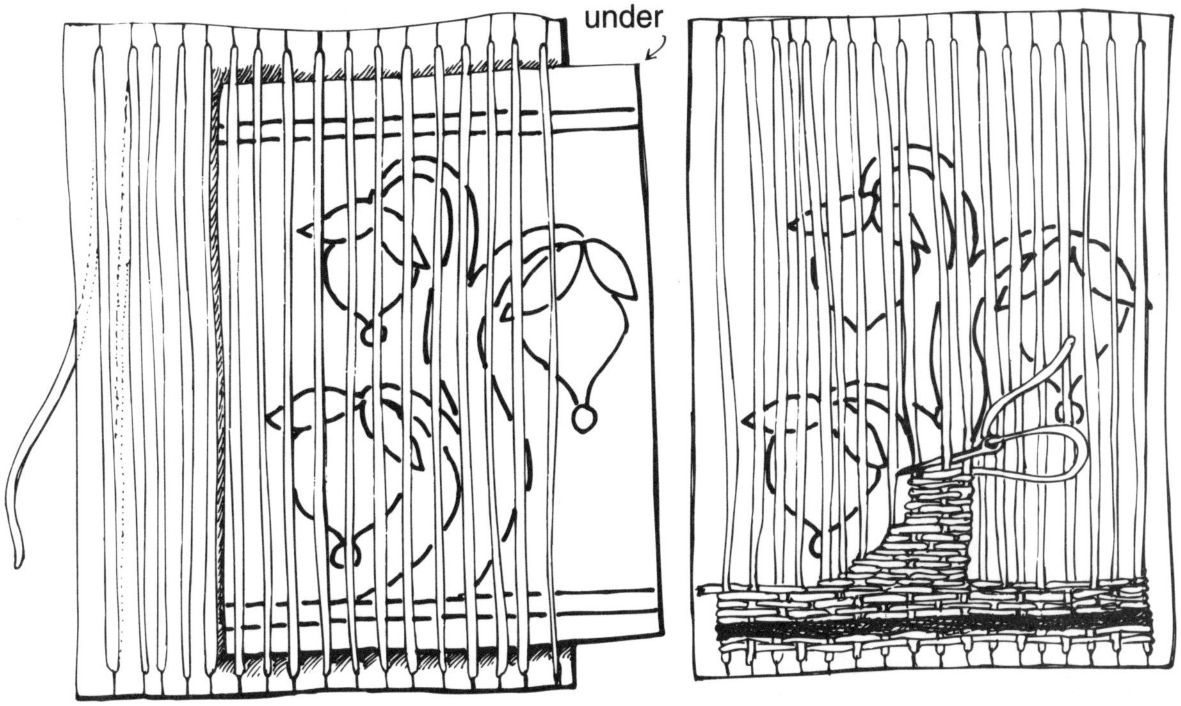
slip sketch
under

Embroidered tapestry

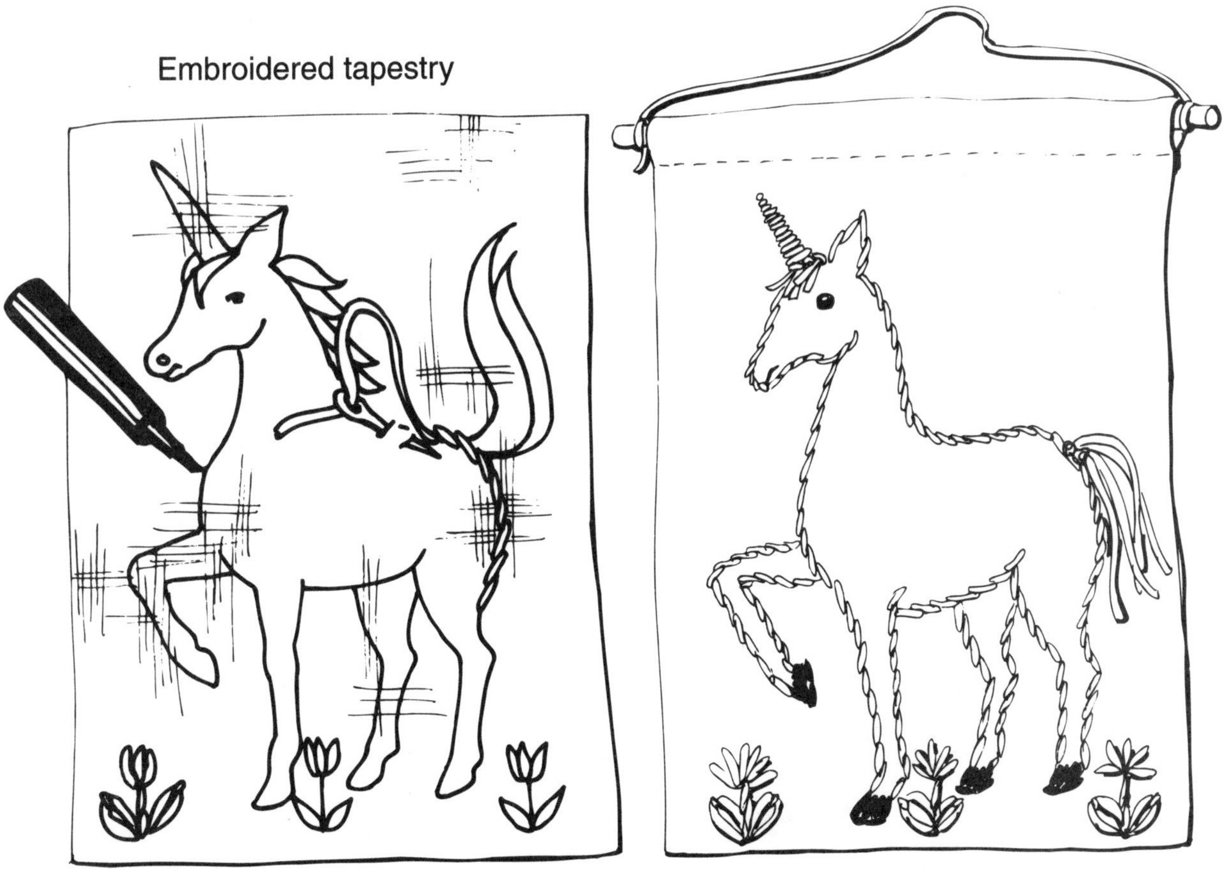

King Arthur and Knights in Shining Armor

King Arthur is often the first character that comes to mind when the Middle Ages are mentioned. With his beautiful Queen Guenevere and his chivalrous knights like Sir Lancelot who sat at his Round Table, the legend is complete. Whether or not a man named Arthur existed at all is unclear. There was, however, a Welsh battle leader by that name during the time when the Romans were in England. Perhaps the legend began there and was embellished as favorite stories often are. What is important is what King Arthur came to represent—the idea of faithfulness, honor, and chivalry. The word "chivalry" comes from the French word "chevalerie" which means simply "horse soldiery." But knights who worked so hard at becoming skilled horsemen also had to adopt a code of honor that befitted knights. Arthur is the most shining example of all that is honorable. His table is round to symbolize that all knights are equal—no one knight sits at the head. Knights were always ready to do battle to protect the honor of their king, their country, or their beloved lady. During battle they donned their shining armor for protection. Originally, armor consisted of a pointed metal helmet and a chain mail shirt. Mail is a kind of "cloth" made by coiling wire around a cylinder, cutting down through one side to form links, and hooking the links together. A tunic of cloth was usually worn over the mail. This armor was sufficiently strong to fend off blows made by the enemies' weapons at the Battle of Hastings as shown in the Bayeux Tapestry. However, as weapons became more advanced and deadly, armor had to be redesigned to provide greater and greater protection until a knight was clad head to toe in heavy steel plates. Horses were bred for strength and size to support this massive weight as well as a little armor of their own.

Though armor was designed for protection, its lines were also affected by the fashions of the period, especially when it was used in tournaments rather than actual warfare. If the fashion of the day was pointed-toe shoes, the steel boots in a suit of armor became pointed. At other times, the toes may have been square. When fashions became more ornate and decorated, this trend was also reflected the "fashion" of armor!

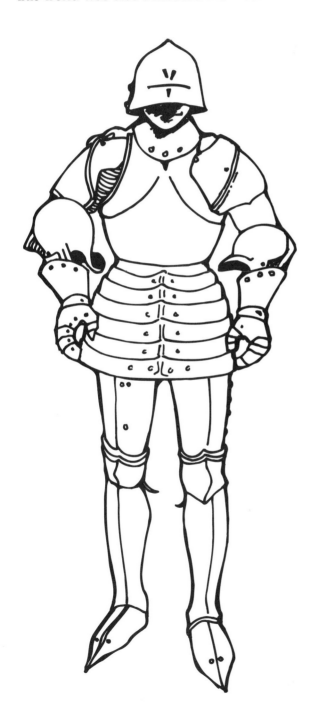 

Activities and Projects

Clad a knight in shining armor. Study the examples of armor shown below and elsewhere in books about the Middle Ages. Draw some sketches until you are pleased with your design. On a large sheet of heavy paper, trace a classmate who will become a knight, or use a copy machine to enlarge the pattern shown below to the size you desire. Spray an old bulky knit sweater with silver spray paint. Cut it and glue it to your figure with white glue or hot glue to

represent chain mail. Recycled aluminum pie and coffee cake pans can be cut easily to create breast plates, knee plates, boots, swords, shields, etc. Be careful of the sharp edges. Wrap aluminum foil around small beans or small newspaper wads to use as rivets that held the armor together. Use cloth or colored paper to create details that are not steel. Cut out a colored photograph of a face proportional to your knight from a magazine and glue the eyes so that they peek out from behind the visor. When the knight is entirely dry, cut him out, knight him "Sir _____" with a thwack on each shoulder as Arthur would have done, and stand him near the door to guard the fortress.

Tournaments and Heraldry

Knights and would-be knights practiced their skills constantly so that they were always ready for battle, but when there was no battle to be fought, mock-battles were often held. Originally these tournaments were almost as dangerous as real battles, with many knights injured and killed. The church tried unsuccessfully to ban this practice in the early thirteenth century and refused Christian burial to anyone who died in this practice. Gradually, however, safety measures were adopted—blunt, non-lethal weapons replaced real ones, strict rules were enforced, and the tournaments became a spectator sport. Though a knight's life was no longer in as much danger, his wealth was. The loser was expected to yield his armor, horse, and equipment to the winner.

Tournaments were festive occasions attended by all. There were many sideshows such as puppet shows and entertainers called minstrels. Minstrels traveled from place to place and spread news in the form of poems put to music telling of the brave deeds of various knights on the battlefield. Knights and lords would pay these performers well to ensure that their stories would be told in a favorable light.

The excitement of a tournament was enhanced by the colorful clothing worn by the participants. Each knight's clothing bore his coat of arms. In order to be recognized as a friend or a foe on the battlefield or at the tournament when they were covered with armor, the knights had emblems or coat of arms sewn onto their tunics and repeated on their shields and other equipment—even their horses. At first these were random designs, whatever struck the creator's fancy, but they gradually became consistent, fixed, adopted by each family, and passed down from generation to generation. Each family's coat of arms reflected a characteristic of the family. Edward III's had a lion to represent England, and to this he added a Fleur-de-Lis, the symbol of France, when he laid claim to the French throne. The practice of tracing genealogies and designing coats of armor is known as heraldry.

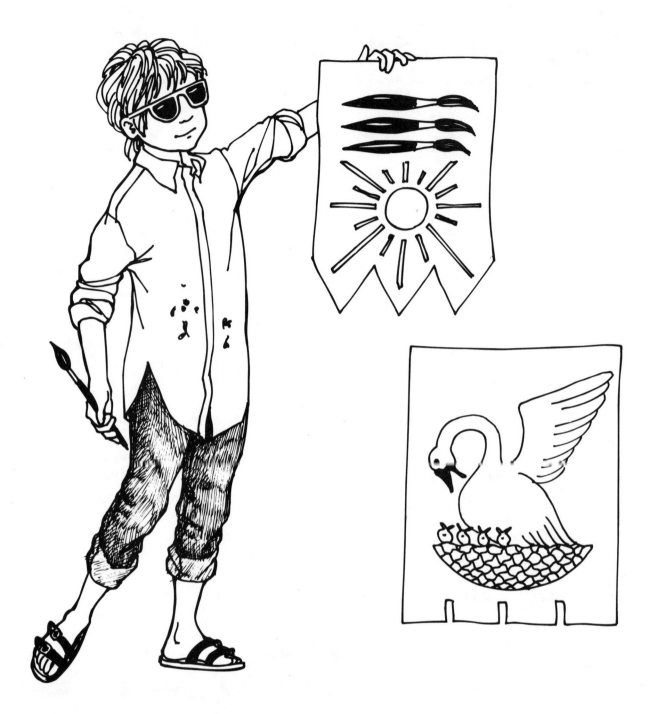

Activities and Projects

Design your own coat of arms. Study those shown above and on page 57, and look in reference books to find others. Some of the designs are simple and geometric, while others are quite complex. Think of images that could symbolize you and your family—interests, talents, occupations of ancestors and so on. Sketch the images. When you are satisfied with your efforts, enlarge and transfer your design onto a shield shape which has been cut from a stiff piece of cardboard or mat board. Or enlarge it on a cloth or paper banner shape such as

those that may hang festively at a tournament. Finish your coat of arms using acrylic paint which will work on paper, cardboard, or cloth. (Tempera may be substituted if you have selected paper for your project.)

Write a paragraph explaining your completed coat of arms so that your classmates can understand why you selected the images you did.

Illuminated Manuscripts and Calligraphy

The first half of the Middle Ages is sometimes referred to as the Dark Ages, partly because of the devastation caused by frequent invasions of armed raiders from the north, such as the Vikings, and also because the vast majority of the populace was kept in the darkness of ignorance. The monks in the monasteries of the church were the only protectors of learning and literature. In their writing rooms, which were called *scriptoriums*, they carefully and silently hand-copied precious volumes including Bibles, gospels, and even the great works of pagan Roman authors for monasteries, churches, and wealthy scholars. These books were not made up of words only, as printed books are today—they were works of art in themselves. Each page was beautifully designed and illustrated, or illuminated. Interestingly enough, many of the designs were inspired by the barbarians from the north, with dragons, birds, or sea monsters intricately twisted around the pages, especially the first letter of each passage.

Later in the Middle Ages, craftsmen outside the church took up the bookmaking trade. At this time, books lavishly illustrated with religious themes and scenes from everyday medieval life were created for kings, queens, nobles, and the very rich.

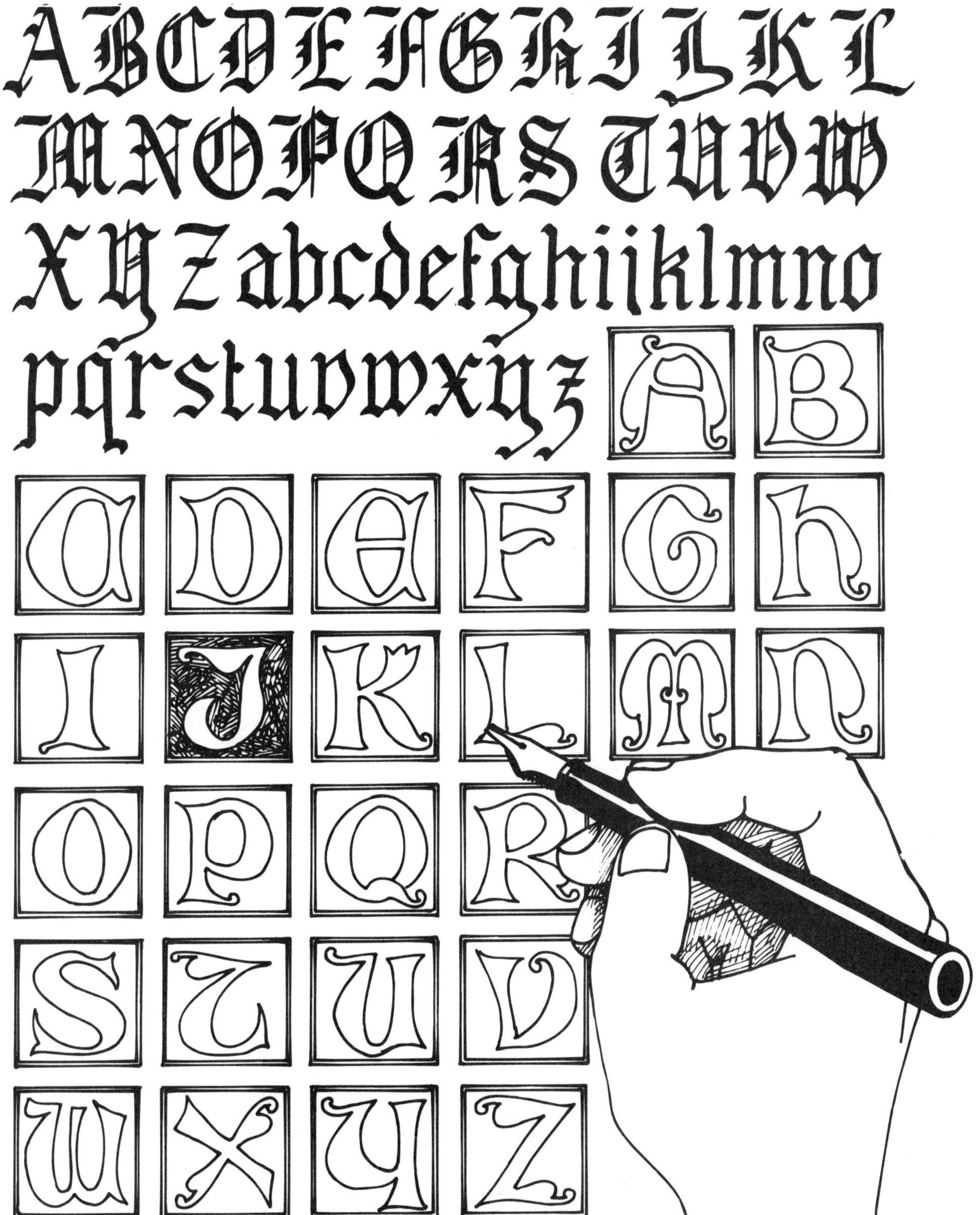
ABCDEFGHIJKL
MNOPQRSTUVW
XYZ abcdefghiijklmno
pqrstuvwxyz
AB
CDEFGH
IJKLMN
OPQR
STUV
WXYZ

Activities and Projects

Select a short passage from a favorite poem or song and illuminate it. Practice the Old English lettering shown on page 59 for the text of your passage. Graph paper makes excellent practice paper because you can be sure both your horizontal and vertical lines are straight. This type of lettering is commonly done using a special flat tipped pen. You can purchase a felt tip variety of such a pen inexpensively. There are also calligraphy sets available with tips or "nibs" in several sizes that use ink cartridges and some that require India ink.

On sketch paper that is the same size the finished piece is to be, lay out your chosen passage. Designate a large square area for the initial letter, and the remainder of the letters can be nestled around it. Use the letters in the boxes on page 59 for the basic shape of the initial letter and embellish it with swirls, flora, fauna, dragons, unicorns, or whatever other image that is appropriate to your subject matter. Select a sheet of parchment paper for the final copy. Paper through which light passes in an antique white or beige color works best. Make sure your hands are perfectly clean. (Some artists and photographers wear thin cotton gloves to avoid fingerprints.) Position the sheet over the sketch and tape the two sheets together in two or three places. Using a light board, or holding the work up to the window, lightly transfer the drawing onto the parchment using a pencil. Complete the finished copy, black letters, and outlines first, then color the illustrations. If possible, use gold paint as this was often used in the Middle Ages. Frame the manuscript or add it to a class book of illuminated manuscripts.

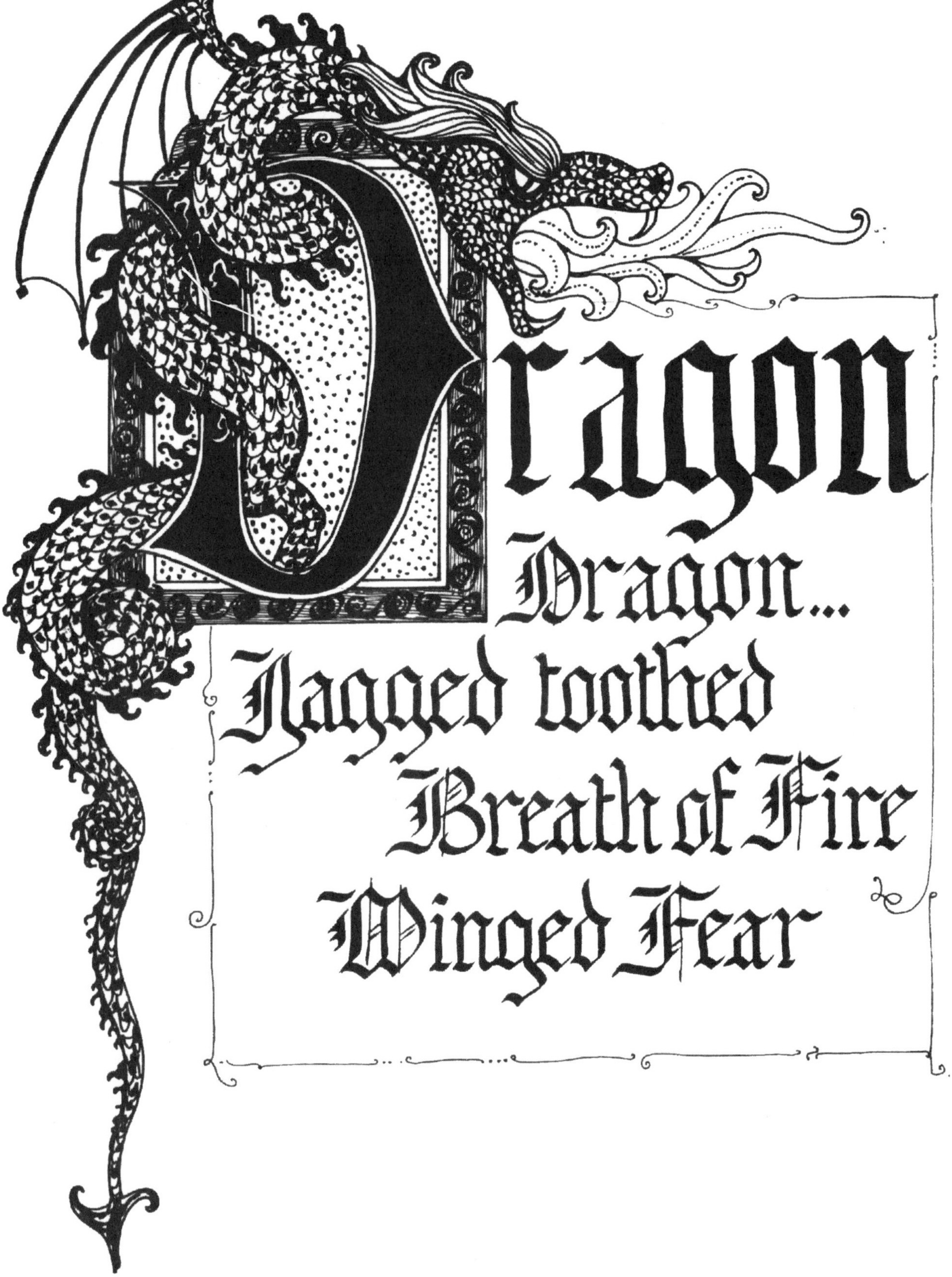
Dragon
Dragon...
Jagged toothed
Breath of Fire
Winged Fear

Gothic Style in Cathedrals and Painting

As the Middle Ages progressed, a major change took place in the architecture of churches. During the 800s to the 1100s, places of worship were built in the Romanesque style, with round arches, thick walls, and columns erected close together. Heavy stone walls surrounded and supported the arched passageways making the interiors dark and damp. In the latter part of the Middle Ages (1100s to 1400s), Gothic architecture became prominent. Pointed arches, thinner walls, and incredibly beautiful stained glass were prominent. The effect was heavenly! The spiritual feeling produced by cathedrals such as Notre Dame in Paris (the word cathedral means throne of the bishop) was very much in keeping with the importance placed on religion at this time.

The Romanesque style of the first part of the Middle Ages had already changed people's thinking about the purposes of art. Gone were attempts to portray the human form as a perfect physical specimen as the ancient Greeks and Romans did. Man's spiritual perfection was considered more important. Folds of robes became stiff, convoluted design elements rather than realistic drapings over living forms. This thinking still affected the way later Gothic artists designed sculptures and stained glass windows for their new cathedrals. Though the windows themselves were huge to fit into the spaces between the arches, they were actually made up of many tiny pieces of colored glass, cut to fit together like a jigsaw puzzle and held with strips of lead.

Activities and Projects

Stained glass is an art form that has enjoyed a revival of popularity in recent years. The creation process involves a great deal of time and expense, and requires handling glass with razor sharp edges as well as caustic materials. If there is an artist who works in this medium in your area, see if it is possible to arrange a visit to his/her workshop. Then using the knowledge gained from such a visit, the example shown below, and other examples from your research at the library, design a stained glass piece of your own. First make a few thumbnail (small) sketches of your ideas. Keep your design simple. It should resemble a page from a child's coloring book. Enlarge your design onto a sheet of paper the actual size of the finished piece. Wrap black electrical tape around the edges of a piece of inexpensive window glass (most glass dealers will cut it to your specifications). Lay your sketch underneath the glass and trace over the lines with a black china marker. Cut out tissue paper to fit the individual shapes of the design and lay them on the sketch to be sure they all fit and the colors are arranged nicely. It is possible to overlap tissue if desired to create different colors. Using a can of glossy spray varnish, spray a small portion of the glass (the side without the china marker) and immediately lay the tissue paper onto the varnished glass surface, smoothing it down with your fingers. **Note:** Be sure to use the spray in a well-venitlated area. Repeat this process until all the tissue pieces are down and spray one more coat over the entire surface.

When the tissued glass has dried completely, go over the lines of your design with permanent marker to resemble the glass leading used in authentic stained glass. Display the finished "faux" stained glass window against a real window for the full transparent effect.

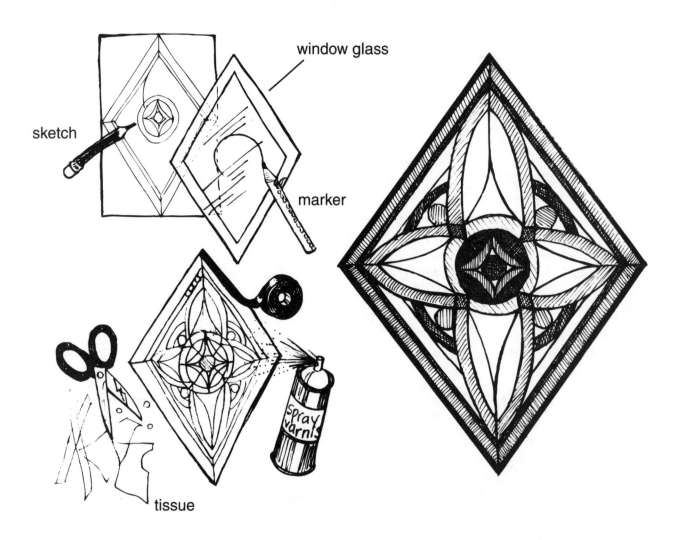

sketch

window glass

marker

tissue

The Renaissance

Life was hard in the Middle Ages. Most of mankind was poor and lived under constant threat of ruthless barbarians who ripped through villages destroying all in their paths and deadly plagues which were known to wipe out as many as one-third of the population. However, during the later years of this period, seeds of progress were planted that would flourish and change the world forever.

One of the seeds was trade. Merchants such as Marco Polo traveled the known world and returned with unusual and beautiful goods and unbelievable tales of strange-looking animals and plants and sophisticated and cultured societies with new and innovative ideas. The people in Europe were hungry to know more.

Trade also brought great wealth. With wealth the arts could thrive. The Italian city-states each tried to outdo one another resulting in many of the finest works of art ever produced. The printing press was invented, so books were available to those who never before even hoped to afford them. Interest in Greek and Roman philosophic literature was revived.

The more new ideas, inventions, and art that people were exposed to, the greater was their desire to know and understand the world around them. The period of the rebirth of this desire for knowledge was perhaps the most exciting time in the history of mankind—the Renaissance.

Observations of a Traveling Man

Merchants traveled around Europe along trade routes that connected the developing towns. Some traveled to the Middle East and traded with Arabs who brought such precious items as silk, pearls, and pepper from India and the Far East on ships. Others went east by an overland route known as the Great Silk Road. Marco Polo was one such merchant who left Venice in 1271. He traveled all over Asia, including Malaysia, Burma, and Indochina in the service of the great Mongol emperor, Kublai Khan. When he returned to Venice after about 24 years, the tales he told of his journeys were so fantastic that people had trouble believing him.

Eventually, the Ottoman Turks took over Constantinople, blocking nearly all trade with the East. The exotic goods and spices that the rich people of Europe desired became rare and very expensive.

Christopher Columbus thought he could avoid the Turks to the east by sailing west around the world until he reached the Indies from the other direction. He finally convinced King Ferdinand and Queen Isabella of Spain to finance his venture in 1492. Though he died thinking he had reached the Japanese Islands and found the new route, he had actually reached the West Indies and stumbled on a whole new world! He returned to Europe with some tales of strange people and unusual plants and animals.

Hearing about other places broadened the horizons of the populations and made them more interested in the world around them. Unlike artists of the Middle Ages who were concerned primarily with the spiritual meaning in their artwork, Renaissance artists such as Leonardo da Vinci wanted to represent the world more realistically and felt that thorough knowledge of nature was essential in order to accomplish this. He had a roomful of botanical specimens and studied and sketched all forms of flora and fauna (plants and animals). He even dissected human corpses to see how the muscles and bones look and worked.

Activities and Projects

Observe and record the real world. Collect some specimens of flora and fauna that are of interest to you. You may even have access to an exotic plant from the florist or an animal specimen from the pet shop or zoo. Sketch at least one of the items from various angles on a sheet of tan or cream paper, or use handmade paper (see pages 74 and 75). As you work, pay careful attention to every detail. It is more important for the finished product to show your understanding of the specimen than to look beautiful. If you are drawing a plant or flower, slice the blossom and draw a close-up of the seeds forming. In the margins make small notes of your observations and conclusions about the specimen.

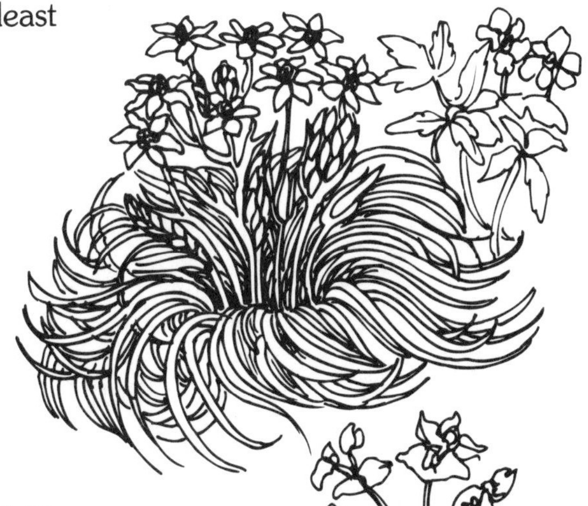

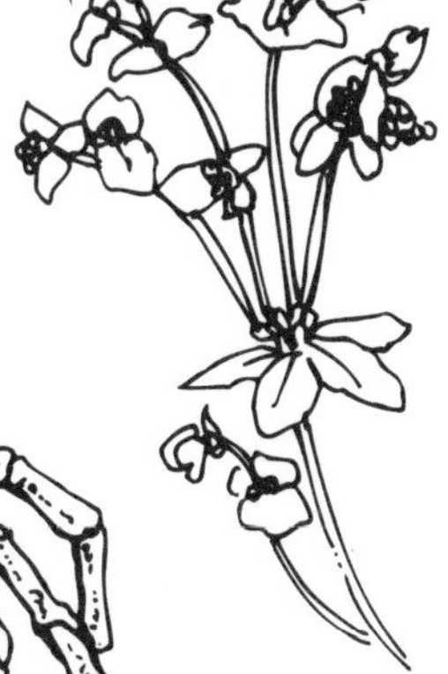

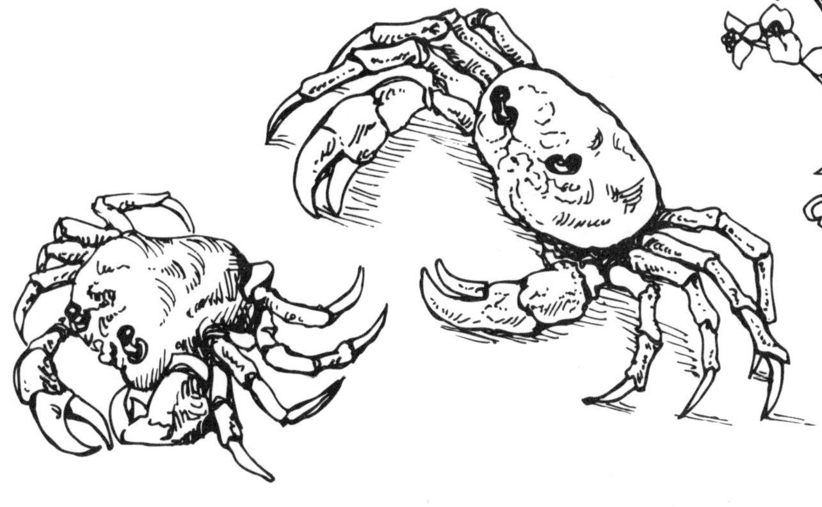

Humanism and the Smiling Woman

During the Renaissance, there was revived appreciation in the knowledge and teachings of the ancient Greeks. They studied what philosophers like Plato had to say about mankind's place in the world and his relationship to nature. This interest in earthly things is reflected in the art that was produced. Artists moved away from the golden backgrounds of the Middle Ages and began to explore how they could make their paintings appear three-dimensional. Jan Van Eyck (pronounced *yon van ike*), a Flemish painter who discovered the technique of

Illustrator's sketch of Leonardo da Vinci's *Mona Lisa*

painting with oils, began including background landscapes to his masterpieces. His ideas spread to Italy. Artists carefully observed nature and studied how light and darks played off figures and landscapes. They saw that the farther away a thing was, the lighter it appeared, and that's how they painted it, using a technique called atmospheric perspective.

Leonardo da Vinci was one of the many famous Renaissance artists who employed this technique. His famous painting, *Mona Lisa*, which today hangs in the Louvre Museum in Paris, has background which recedes far into the distance. The figure herself was also painted in a fresh, new way. Da Vinci used a technique called *sfumato* which created depth and roundness by gradually building up thin, nearly transparent layers of glazes, one on top of the other, so that Mona Lisa's face seemed to glow from within. Da Vinci's peers were intrigued by this new technique and by the mysterious smile on her face, which still affects all those who see her, making this simple portrait one of the most famous paintings ever.

Activities and Projects

Work in the Renaissance tradition to create a mysterious smiling woman of your own. Study da Vinci's *Mona Lisa* carefully (if you can't fly to Paris to see her, a color reproduction will do). Find examples of atmospheric perspective and rounded figures by other artists of the period such as Raphael, Michelangelo, Botticelli, Titian, and Bellini. With these great artist's works as inspiration and your own careful outside observation, begin a landscape background. Use tempera paint or chalk pastels on a 20" x 30" sheet of paper (approximate size of the Mona Lisa). Begin with the sky, working from the top down and blending blue, aqua, and white paint or chalk so that the sky gets gradually lighter. When you have reached about a fourth of the way down your paper, use blue or purple to add a faint, not quite flat horizon line. Continue working downward, making the colors gradually darker. The palest part of your picture should be the horizon, because it is farthest away.

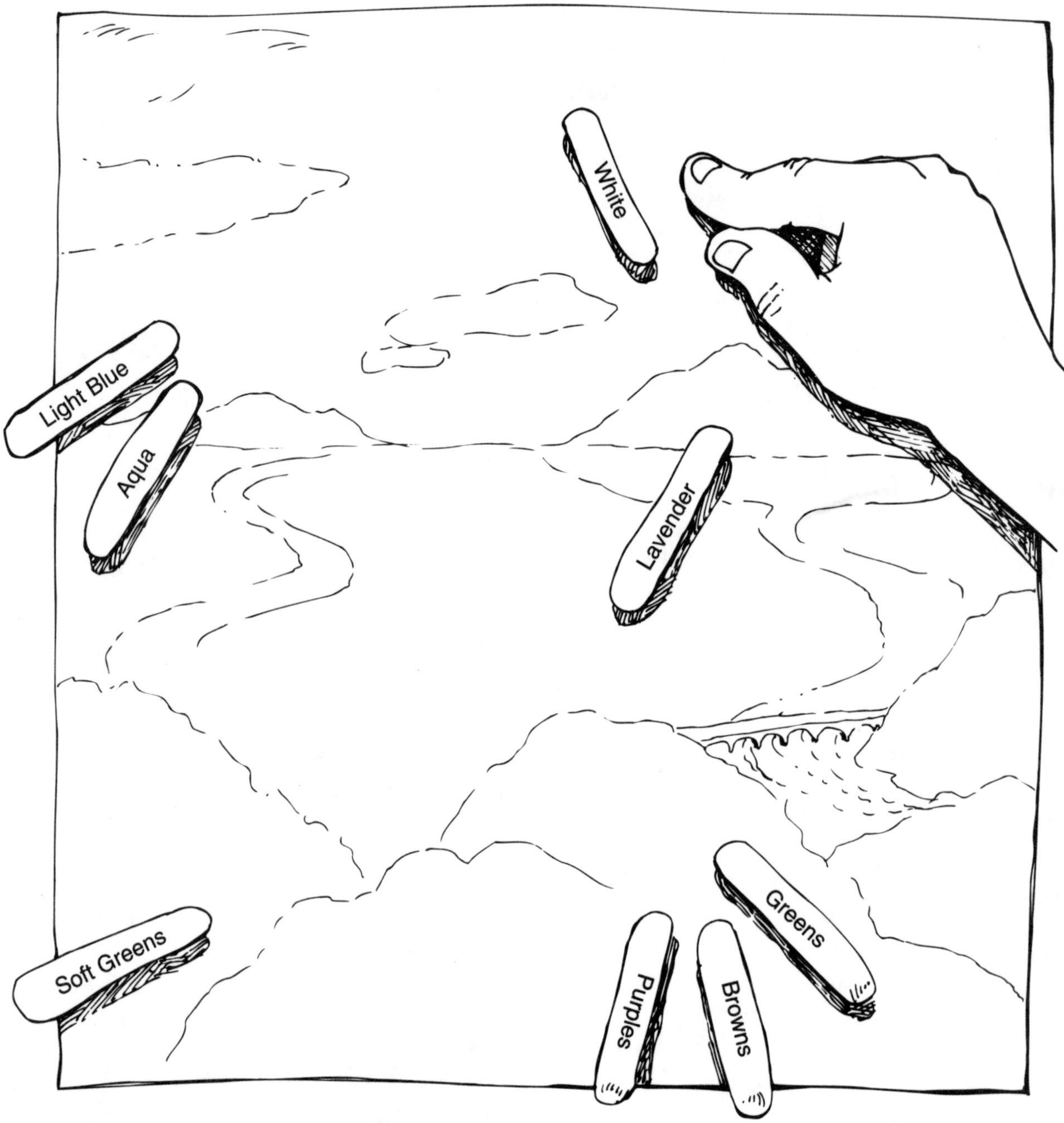
White
Light Blue
Aqua
Lavender
Soft Greens
Greens
Purples
Browns

You may choose to draw pale, purple mountains, winding streams or roads, trees and shrubs, even far off figures, but you needn't add too many details to the center part of the picture as you will be covering that portion with your figure.

Begin the figure on a separate sheet of paper. The paper should be the same size as the background or a little smaller. Refer to the Renaissance works and then look at people around you. Note those things which are similar in all faces and also note the differences. Most all faces are basically egg-shaped and bilaterally symmetrical (the same on both sides). Eyes are located along a line that cuts the egg in half horizontally. The space between the

Egg-shaped head, divided in half lengthwise and crosswise
Wavy hair follows contours of head, so does veil
Eyes halfway down, football shape. Lids and brows follow same curve, irises are circles with top behind lid
Hair looks darker in the shadows near the neck
Folds in robes follow body contours
Cut the figure out, and glue to background

eyes is usually about an eye's width, but each person's eyes are a different color, size, and shape, with individual eyelids, creases, and lashes. The same holds true for the rest of the figure. Using your greatest powers of observation in the same manner that da Vinci did, sketch an egg-shape the size of an actual head, then complete the face as shown. If you don't trust your eyes, measure distances between features with a ruler and transfer the measurements onto your paper. When you have completed the drawing lightly in pencil, use chalk in various shades and blend it into the face to make it appear rounded. Finish by adding hair and garments. Then cut around the outline of your figure and glue it to the background you prepared previously.

A New Perspective

While atmospheric perspective worked well in making painted landscapes appear to recede in space, buildings were another problem. Medieval artists tried rather clumsily to represent them effectively, but it was not until the early 1400s that Filippo Brunelleschi solved this problem by inventing a system called *linear perspective*—a mathematical means to make buildings painted on a flat surface appear three-dimensional. This technique employs a vanishing point, which is that place near the horizon where two parallel lines seem to converge like the rails of a train track on a flat ground. Paolo Uccello loved linear perspective. He drew detailed studies of geometric objects and painted mainly for the purpose of showing off his great skill and knowledge of perspective. The swords in his famous painting, *Battle of San Romano*, all seem to have fallen in a perfect grid, which would never happen in real life. He painted many horses in this picture from various angles and also employed a technique called *foreshortening* to achieve the appearance that the horses are facing the viewer head on or lying dead on the ground.

Activities and Projects

Create a three-dimensional work of art. Study examples of linear perspective in paintings by such Renaissance artists as Paolo Uccello, Filippo Brunelleschi, or Masaccio who employed this newly discovered technique. Then try your hand at this technique by painting a three-dimensional chessboard. You will need a yardstick, pencil, eraser, and a sheet of heavy drawing or watercolor paper 18- or 20-inches square. Draw a baseline across the bottom of the paper to form the front of the grid. Add nine small marks at two-inch intervals so that there are eight spaces. Add a small dot in the middle of the top of the paper. This is the vanishing point. Pressing lightly with your pencil so the guidelines can later be erased, connect each of the nine marks to the vanishing point to create parallel lines that appear to recede into the background. Draw another horizontal line halfway up the page to represent the back edge of the grid. Dividing the stripes into squares is the trickiest part. Begin by drawing two diagonal lines from opposite corners. Where these two lines cross is the center of the board. Draw a horizontal line across the grid through that point. In this manner, find the center of the back half of the grid, then the front half. You have now divided the grid into four equal parts. Divide each of the four parts once more, and your grid is complete with eight squares across and eight squares down. The illustration on page 73 should help you through this complicated process. Erase all the guidelines, then choose your favorite color and paint every other square, like a chessboard. If you use watercolors for this process, drop another color onto each square while it is still wet for an interesting mottled effect. Another way to create interest is to sprinkle a few grains of salt onto the wet paint. When you have finished with one color, select a contrasting color for the other squares and repeat the process.

When your three-dimensional chessboard is completely dry, cut it out, and mount it on a clean sheet of paper. Draw and cut out at least three chess pieces of your design, perhaps in Renaissance dress. Try to use the technique of foreshortening as shown in the examples below. Be sure to make the pieces different sizes, gluing the smaller ones in place near the back of the chessboard because they are farther away and the larger ones near the front. If you have access to a photocopy machine which will enlarge and reduce, this last step could be achieved by photocopying a figure from a Renaissance painting in a book, cutting away the background and enlarging or reducing it so that it fits the chessboard. Be sure the chess pieces are colored.

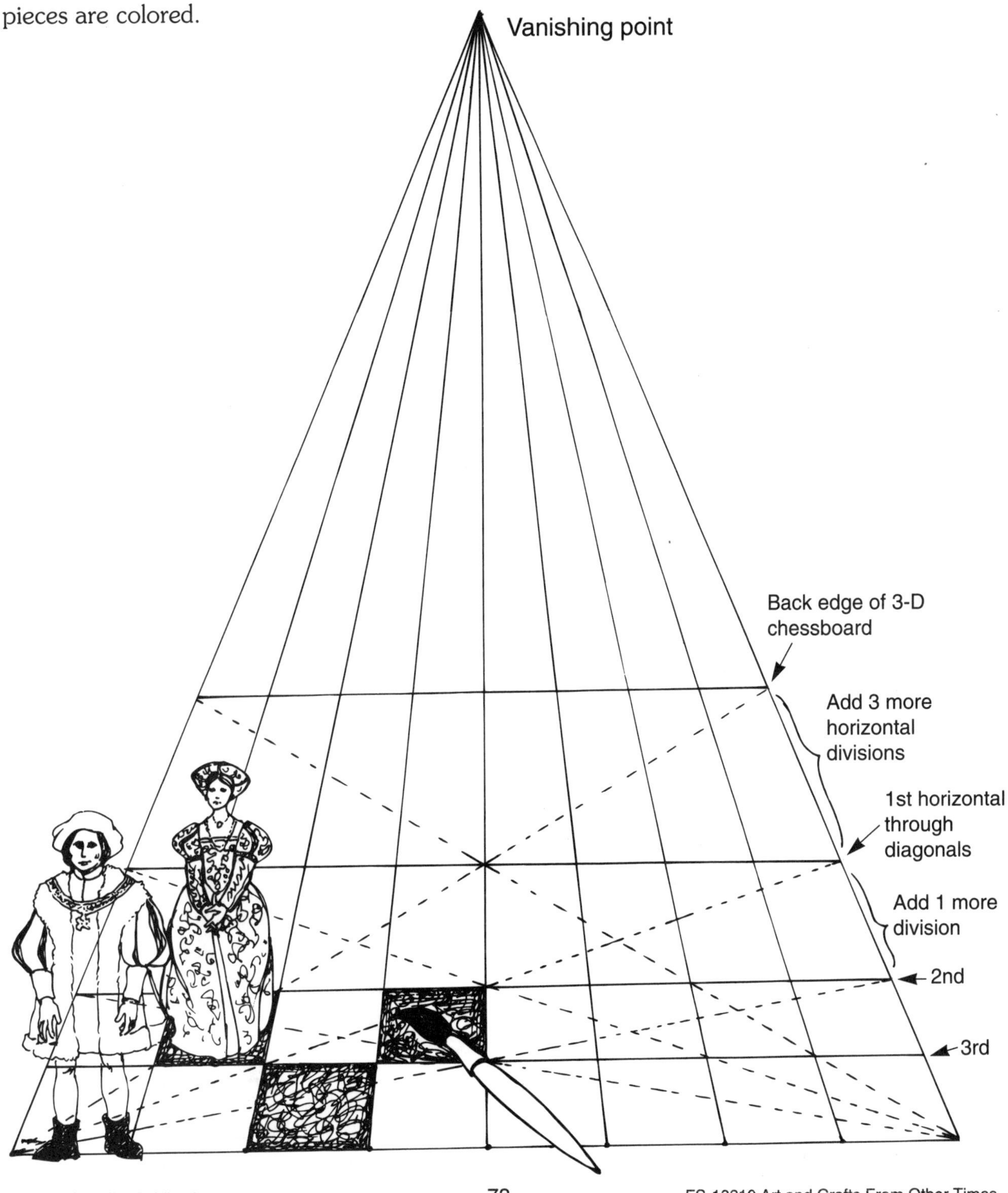

Vanishing point
Back edge of 3-D chessboard
Add 3 more horizontal divisions
1st horizontal through diagonals
Add 1 more division
2nd
3rd

The Printed Word

The Renaissance may never have happened at all if it had not been for Johannes Gutenberg who invented the printing press. He knew how to cast metal from his uncle who made coins. Around the middle of the 1400s Gutenberg realized that if he made molds of letters in the alphabet all the same size, he could arrange them in a frame to spell words and sentences. He could then ink them, lay a sheet of paper over them, and press down to print them. Once a page was set up, he could make many copies quickly and inexpensively, then reassemble the same letters for the next page. This process made books much cheaper and more people had access to them. It is estimated that in the century following Gutenberg's invention, several million books were printed!

A new technique used in making paper was also developed at that time which made paper, and therefore books, cheaper to manufacture. Old rags were boiled to make a pulp, which was strained through a screen, pressed to remove excess water, then laid flat to dry. This process is still used today to make fine art papers.

Activities and Projects

Make some paper. To do this, make a wooden frame or use an old 9" x 12" picture frame. Cut a piece of screen slightly larger than the frame and staple it into the wood around the edges. Collect recycled paper from the wastebasket, feeder strips from computer paper, napkins, and paper towels. Tear these into approximately one-inch pieces and place them loosely in a blender until it is about half full. Fill the blender halfway with water, and blend the paper scraps until all pieces have been pulverized. Hold the screen frame over a larger roasting pan and carefully pour the pulp mixture over the screen until there is an even layer of pulp about one-quarter-inch thick. Allow excess water to drain into the roasting pan. Then place a thin cotton cloth or old dryer sheet over the drained pulp. Lightly dab the surface with a sponge to remove more water. Invert the paper onto several layers of newspaper or squares of old blankets that are larger than the handmade paper. Cover them with another thickness of blanket. Repeat this

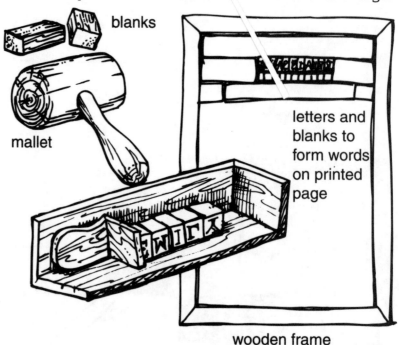

blanks

mallet

letters and blanks to form words on printed page

wooden frame

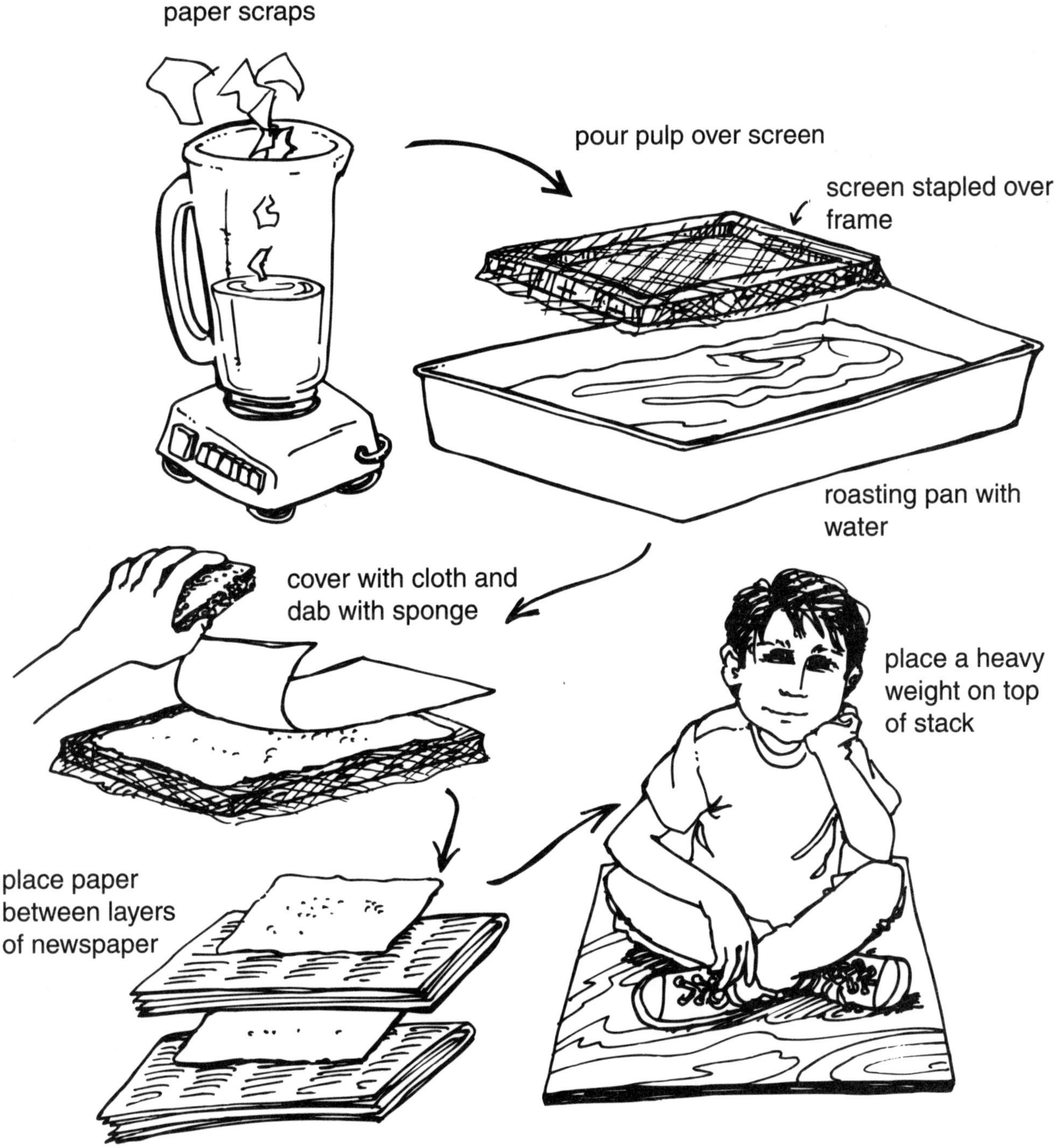
paper scraps
pour pulp over screen
screen stapled over frame
roasting pan with water
cover with cloth and dab with sponge
place a heavy weight on top of stack
place paper between layers of newspaper

process, layering sheet upon sheet until you have made as much paper as you wish. Add a stiff sheet of plywood and weight it down with some heavy books. Remove layers one at a time and allow the paper to finish drying flat.

Use this paper for your botanical drawing (see page 67) or your invention sketches (see page 78).

The Invention Explosion

The printing press put books into the hands of many and the minds of many came alive. Scientists could read about current research and discoveries and begin their studies from there instead of starting from scratch. Alchemists searched for magic substances like one that would turn metal into gold called "Philosopher's Stone" and the "Elixer of Life" so they could live forever. Though they were, of course, not successful, their careful observations and notes not only taught us much about the properties of substances, but also introduced the world to the modern scientific method which we still use today.

Also at this time, mathematicians borrowed ideas from the math scholars in the Middle East and India who were very advanced in their knowledge of algebra. Galileo did many scientific experiments which disproved some things that people had never dared to question. Questioning old ideas was once considered heresy, but during the Renaissance it was encouraged.

With such a positive atmosphere for learning, there was an explosion of inventions. Spring-driven clocks, watches, gunpowder, the thermometer, and the telescope are just a few of the many inventions that were created during the Renaissance. Once again, Leonardo da Vinci's fertile mind was at work. He enjoyed what he called *pre-imagining*, or imagining things before they actually existed. Not only were his notebooks filled with sketches from nature, but also with thousands of pre-imaginings including a parachute, a flying machine, a movable bridge, and a construction crane.

Activities and Projects

Make a class "Invention Notebook." Study the drawings shown on this page and on page 76. Then think of an invention of your own that you think would benefit the world. Maybe you could design a mechanical bath machine complete with hair shampooer and nail clipper, or an automatic studying machine, or trousers that can be programmed to take you anywhere and exercise your legs effortlessly, or a garbage recycling machine that creates energy to run a computer.

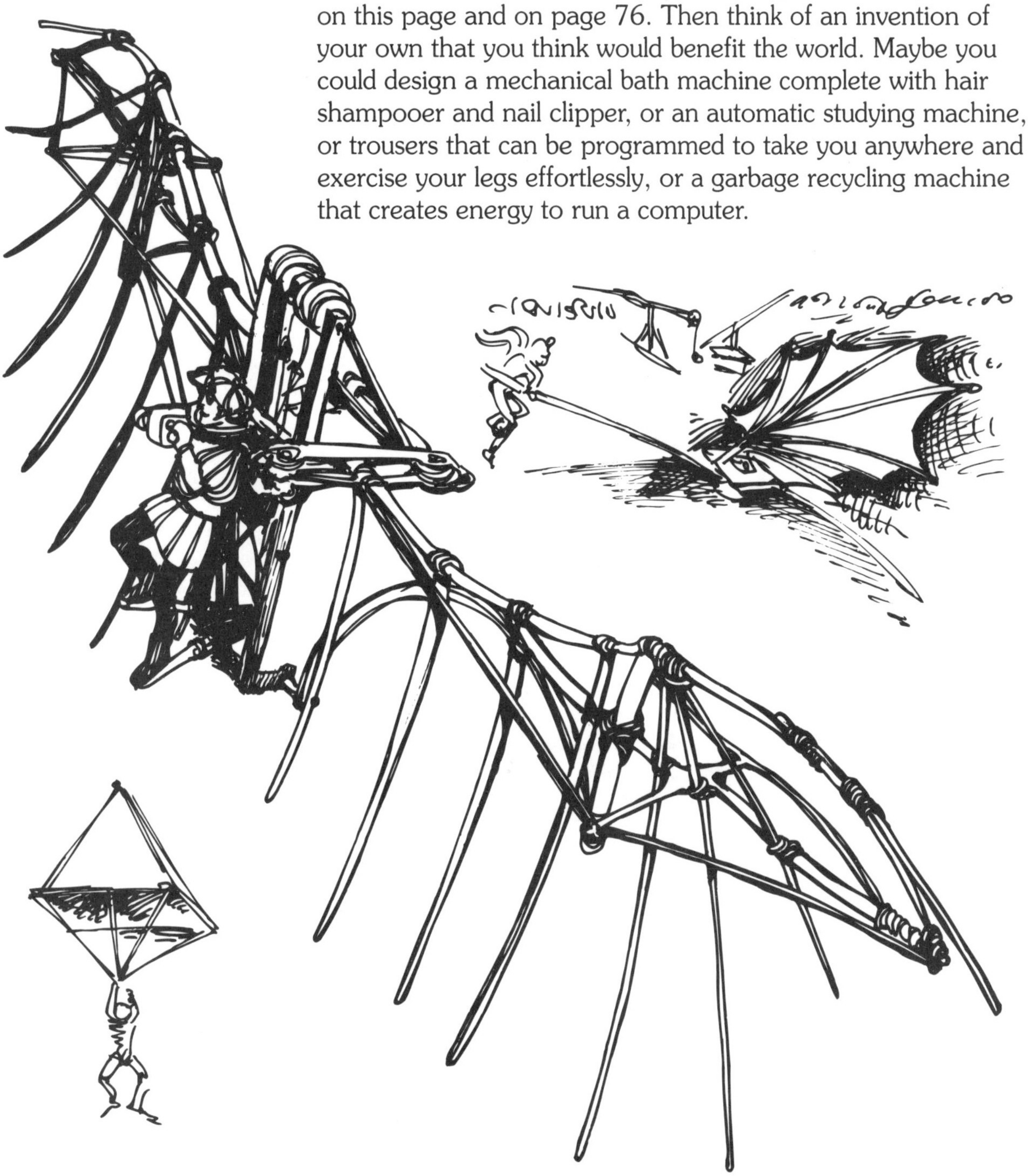

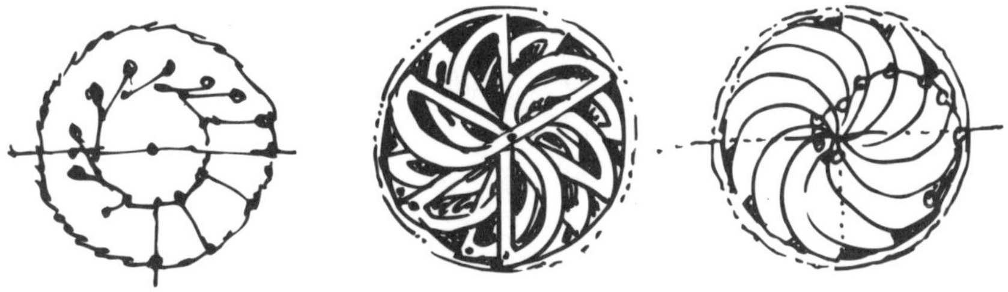

Sketch your ideas on scratch paper and then again in ink using tiny brushes and old-looking or handmade paper (see pages 74 and 75). Be sure to include notes of explanation in the margins. You may want to write the notes backwards, because that is how Leonardo da Vinci wrote his.

Use another sheet of the same paper to make a cover. In fancy, backward letters write "Leonardo's Notebook," or "Da Vinci's Diary," or "The Renaissance of Ideas." Punch holes along the side of each inventive page and lace them all together with yarn or a thin ribbon.

Idea: Use a mirror to help you write or read a backwards note.

Art in the Modern World

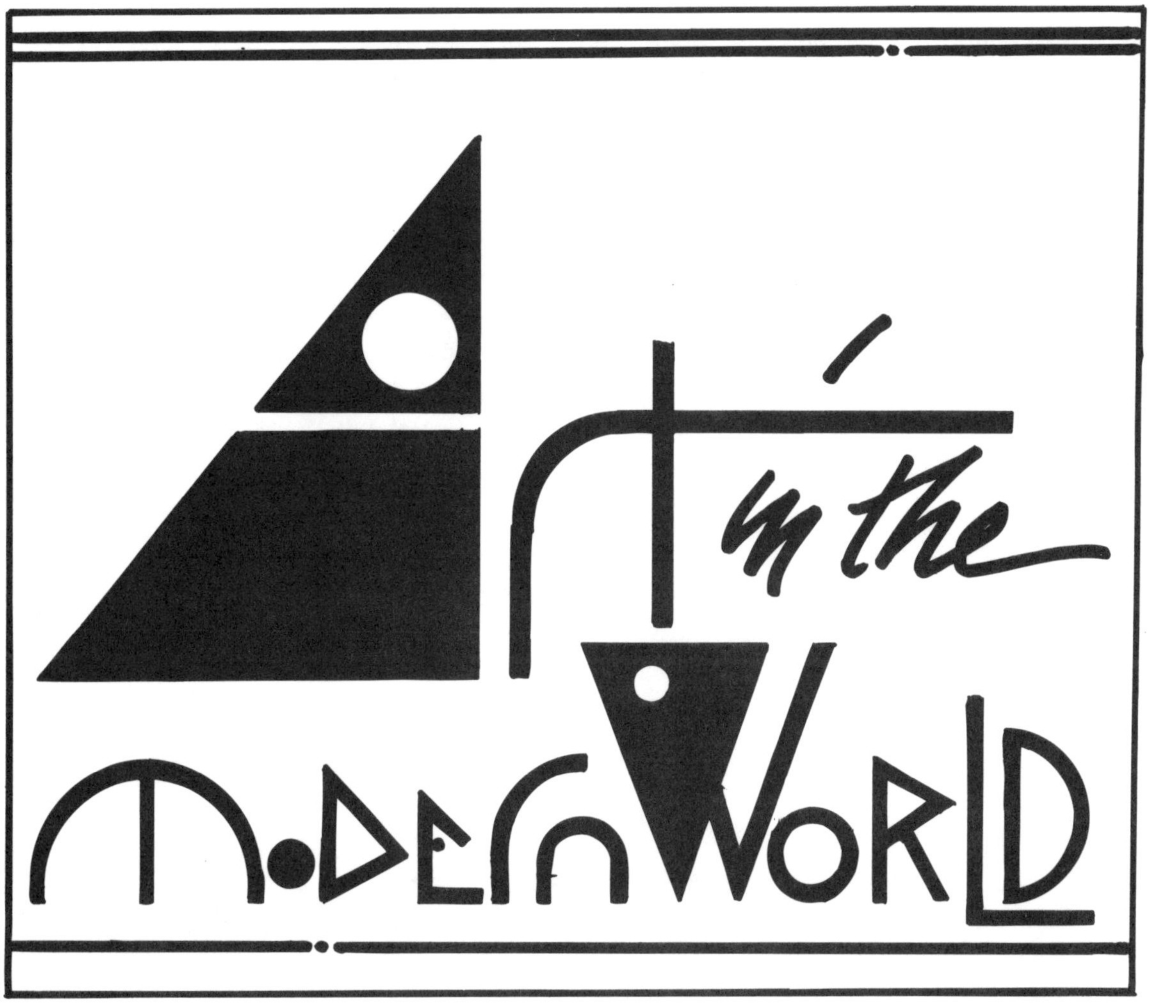
Art in the Modern World

Many people believed the great artists of the Renaissance had achieved all there was to achieve in the world of art. After that enlightened period of rebirth, artists simply strove to copy the masters as closely as they could because there were no higher goals to reach for. These artists carried the art to the extreme by embellishing the embellishments and calling it the Baroque style. But artists, with their creative natures, have never enjoyed copying others for long and gradually artists began to search for alternate directions to explore in the world of creative expression. Some artists began looking to ordinary people rather than to royalty or religious or mythical figures for their subjects. Later, artists left their studios and went outside to paint from nature. How a thing was painted, the artist's style, became more important than what was painted. Some artists felt that the most important aspect of art was the personal relationship an artist has with his or her own art—the right to create whatever he or she pleases, rather than filling the canvas with deep meaning and symbolism to satisfy what society expected. This idea came to be known as "Art for Art's Sake." Art had stepped into the modern world.

Impressionism

Several forces led to the style of art we know as Impressionism. One was called the Barbizon school of painting where artists went outside and painted on location. Two English landscape artists, Constable and Turner, inspired later Impressionists with their beautiful renderings of diffused lighting in their skies. An artist named Boudin captured the sea on canvas as he worked quickly beside it. This resulted in great feeling of spontaneity which impressed one of his students—Claude Monet. Monet and other Impressionists were concerned with carefully depicting how the light that fell on objects affected them and changed their appearance as the light constantly moved across their surfaces. They paid close attention to the colors of reflections of adjacent objects as light bounced off one object to another and also the shadows which they painted in rich purples, blues, and greens. They laid small strokes of a variety of colors next to each other so that they blend visually as we view them. Try it!

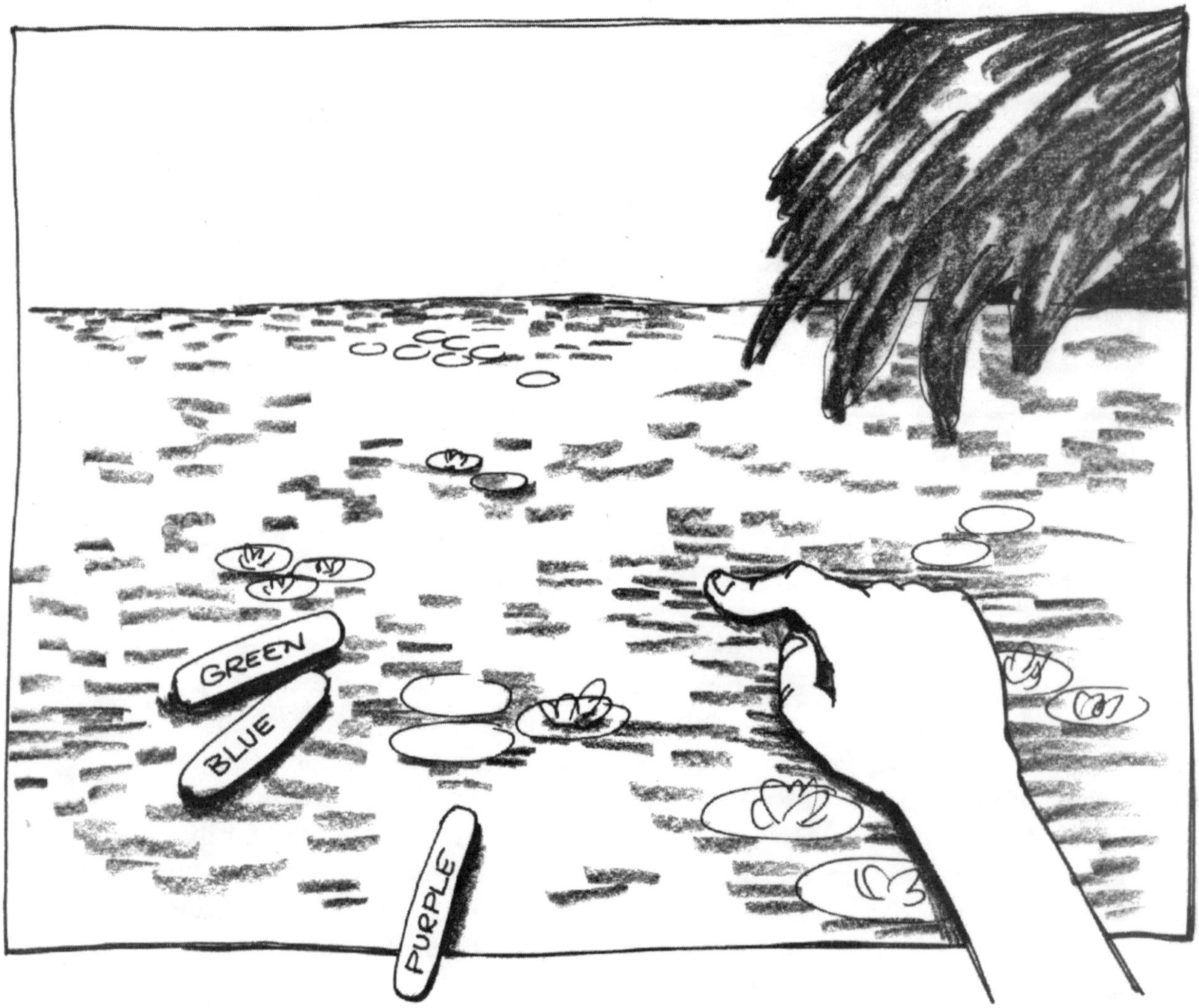
GREEN
BLUE
PURPLE

Impressionist art is still very popular today. People flock to art shows that feature works of Monet and others. What is maybe even more important is the effect it had on the whole world of art. It gave other artists the freedom to explore new directions in art, and they went in all different directions to be sure. Georges Seurat laid complementary colors down in tiny, precise dots, which resulted in a style known as pointillism. Vincent van Gogh used dashes of color like the impressionists, but his goal was to show the feelings different colors could

evoke. Paul Gauguin's direction led him to Tahiti where he painted the shapes of the native plants and people in languid, brilliant colors. Others, like Paul Cezanne, flattened the shapes of the objects they painted into planes and stressed form and mass. This idea grew into the Cubist movement of the early 1900s and involved such artists as Pablo Picasso and Georges Braque. Henri Matisse and his fellow artists distorted shapes, colors, and space so much that an exhibition of their work caused a huge uproar. They were labeled "Fauvists" which means "wild animals," but they were proud of the title!

Activities and Projects

Create an Impressionist work of your own. Study the paintings that Claude Monet did at the famous gardens of Giverny in France. Get very close to one of his paintings of water lilies and note how the color is laid down on the canvas in small areas which all blend together when you move back. Play a recording of "Clair de Lune" by the French Impressionist composer, Claude Debussy, while you dreamily create a quiet, still pond with a few clusters of water lilies floating on it. Use chalk pastels in the same cool colors you identify in Monet's work on blue or white paper that is rough enough to hold onto the chalk when you apply it. Lightly sketch some ovals with a pencil and suggest images of lilies as Monet did. Work in horizontal strokes, placing one color next to and on top of another and see how they blend to make a new color. Include some lighter areas and some patches of darker shades to represent light and shadow. Don't use black. This activity should be so relaxing that once you get into it, be careful to stay awake! To protect your finished work from smearing, spray a light coat of spray fixative (which can be purchased from an art supply store) or use hairspray. Mat your work with white, pale pink, or mauve.

Try your hand at Cubism by creating a self-portrait. Collect several large photographs of yourself. You may need to enlarge them on a copy machine. Cut some faces from articles and advertisements in magazines. Cut all the faces you have gathered into pieces as if they were shattered fragments of a mirror. Lay them around you within easy reach. Select pieces from the fragments and arrange them onto a sheet of heavy paper in roughly the same

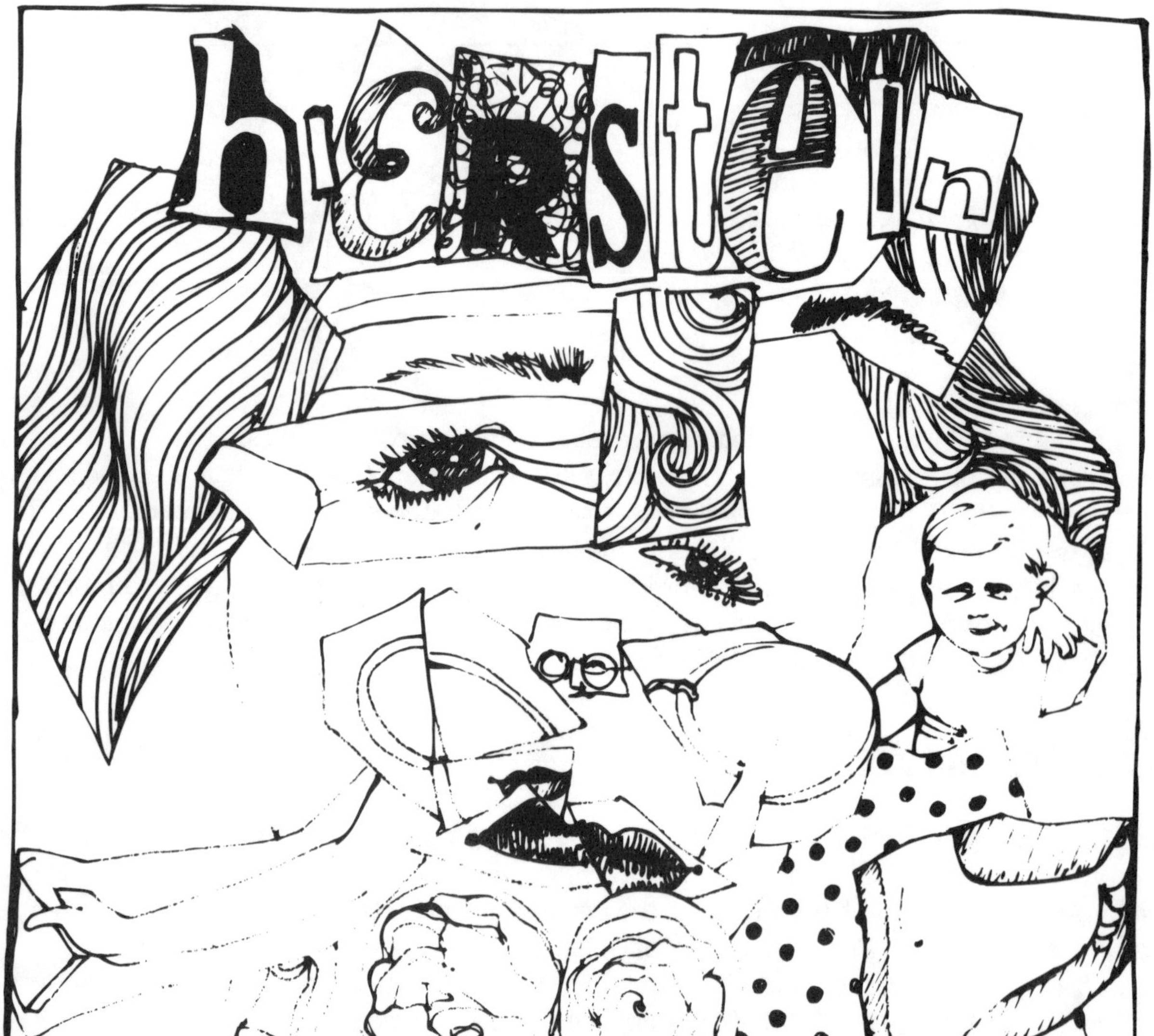
h'ERstein

configuration as an actual face would have, but distorted. You needn't use all of the pieces, just enough to create an interesting Cubist work of art. Glue the pieces into place. You may wish to apply a coat of decoupage medium, acrylic sealer, polyurethane, or thinned white glue to protect the piece once it's complete and to give it an even shine. Be sure that whatever you use will not cause the pieces to smear when you apply the protective coat.

Abstract Art

Cubism was one of the first steps to abstract art. When artists were first exposed to that distorted style, they were inspired to explore their own unique versions of reality. Some, like Russian-born Wassily Kandinsky and Paul Klee from Switzerland, painted detailed abstract shapes and colors that they believed could produce emotion. Others, like Dutch artist Piet Mondrian, painted only pure forms using bright, primary colors within geometric horizontal and vertical lines. His style influenced modern commercial art and industrial design. Later, purely geometric forms were painted so as to create optical illusions for those who viewed them. They were called Op art. Artists like Frank Stella placed complementary colors and other unusual combinations of colors beside one another on the canvas resulting in a visual vibration of the eyes of the viewer. Victor Vasarely painted black and white checkerboards which seem to bubble up from the surface of the work.

Activities and Projects

Do a little geometry yourself. Study the examples of Abstract art and Op art shown on page 84 and in art books. Then make a few thumbnail sketches in an abstract design of your own. When you are satisfied with one of your designs, think about color. You may choose to

Illustrator's drawing in Victor Vasarely's style

work entirely in black and white, or experiment with unusual color combinations placed side by side. Use a ruler and a compass to redraw the sketch onto a large sheet of paper (or canvas). Some abstract art on display in museums is large enough to fill an entire gallery room, and the size of a piece can add to its impact. Work in a size with which you feel comfortable. Artists use several methods to paint their work. They may work in oil paint or acrylics, or they may use masking tape to mask off perfectly straight lines and airbrush or spray paint the piece. Choose one of these options or simply use tempera to complete your abstract work of art. Give it an obscure title.

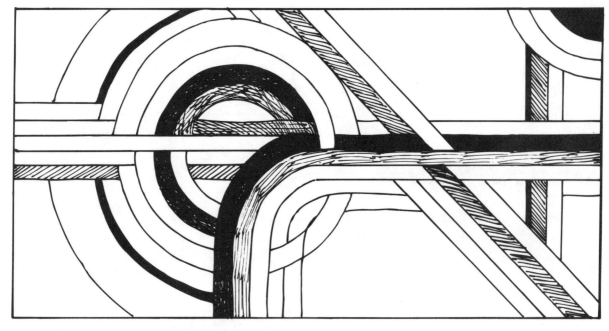

Illustrator's drawing in Frank Stella's style

Abstract Expressionism

Though European art movements were known, accepted, and practiced by some artists in the United States, there was a movement in the 1930s which rebelled against these new styles. It was called American Realism. Thomas Hart Benton, Grant Wood, and Edward Hopper all painted realistic, though somewhat stylized pictures of life in the world around them. Hopper painted lone figures isolated in the big city; Wood and Benton painted the landscapes, folk tales, and legends of the midwest.

During the 1930s and after World War II began in 1939, many European artists moved to the United States. These artists influenced many young American painters, and by 1943 the most significant movement in modern American painting—abstract expressionism—had been created. These artists began to paint totally spontaneous works guided by their subconscious minds. They had an idea that the process they went through in the creation of a piece of art was more important than the finished work itself. This was sometimes referred to as action painting.

Illustrator's sketch of Grant Wood's *American Gothic*

Jackson Pollock began to drip and throw paint onto his canvases. In Morris Louis' *Blue Veil*, the artist stained color into his canvas instead of applying it with a brush. The color was thus an actual part of the painting surface.

Some artists squeezed paint directly from the tube, building it up on the canvas like toothpaste. Some staged "happenings" and rolled through the paint across a canvas. One artist went to airports and threw buckets of color onto huge canvases that had been placed behind jet engines, letting the blast of the engine blow the paint around. Canvases no longer had to be rectangular or flat. Like collage, anything could be glued on and incorporated into the art.

Activities and Projects

Express your subconscious self with an action painting. Study some of the techniques used by the abstract expressionists to apply paint to a canvas. Select a technique that appeals to you. Or invent a whole new method of painting that no one else has thought of yet! Using oil paint, acrylics, tempera, house paint, or spray paint, stand before a blank canvas and see what unfolds. It is strongly suggested that this activity be conducted outside or with an ample supply of drop cloths and newspapers to protect your surroundings.

Smaller versions of all paint applications are possible, and perhaps more practical.

Apply paint by dripping

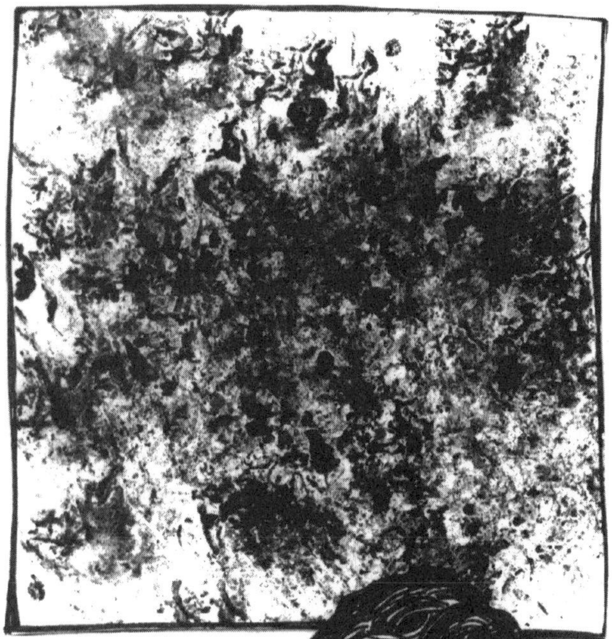

or by rubbing with
a paper towel

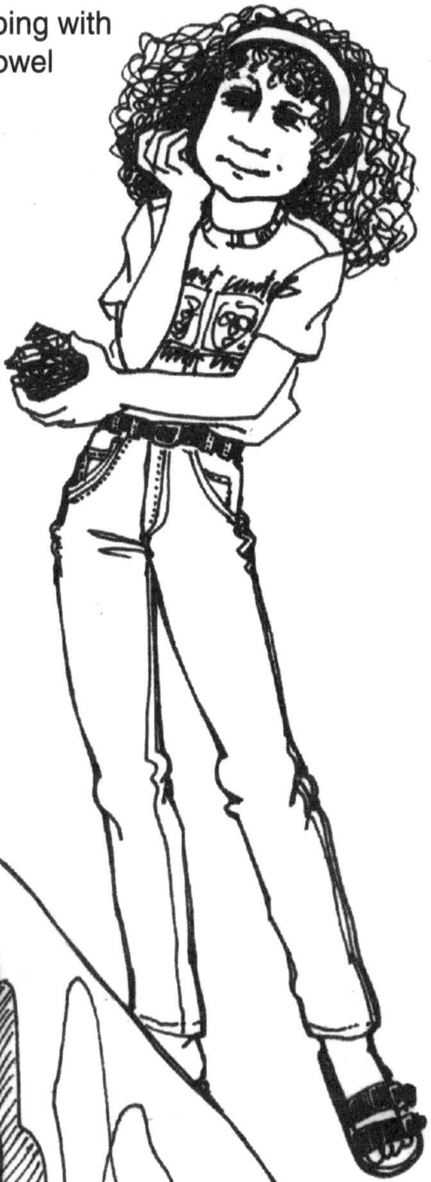

or by pouring

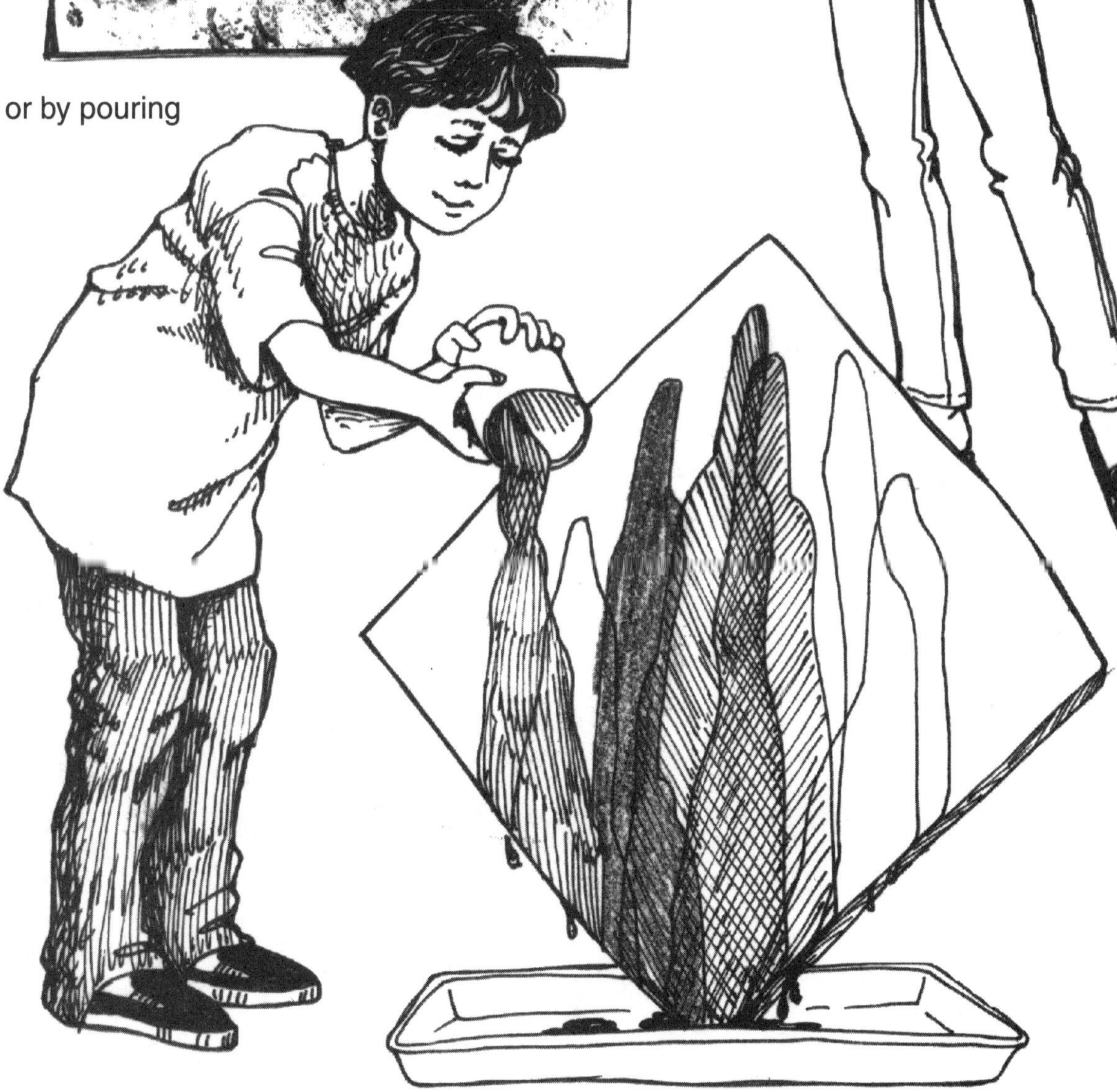

Pop Art

It seems no matter what style of art is currently in vogue, there is always a new movement on the rise that rebels against it. So it was with Pop art (from popular art). Pop artists considered the abstract expressionists too far removed from reality, so they incorporated elements of popular culture into their art. Roy Lichtenstein enlarged comic strips to wall-sized proportions. Jasper Johns did a series of paintings using the American flag as subject matter. Andy Warhol is famous for his silk-screen prints of soup cans, soda pop bottles, and Marilyn Monroe. Pop artists often added pieces of materials from modern technology such as plastic, foam, metal, and glass to their work in the tradition of collage. Claes Oldenburg made huge, crazy sculptures of fast-food items. One of his sculptures—a giant cherry perched on the tip of a spoon—is the focal point in the sculpture garden of the art center in Minneapolis. He also designed many zany sculptures which were never actually meant to be constructed. The idea that the concept was more important than the finished product was termed conceptual art.

Some modern artists have adopted the trend of Photo Realism. Artists of this trend work from photographs to meticulously duplicate subjects from our pop culture such as neon signs and glass store fronts. Often these works are highly complex because they show the subject matter through the window and also the reflections on that window itself.

Activities and Projects

Make a Pop art statement about our culture today. Collect all sorts of scraps and fragments of everyday items such as newspaper and magazine photos showing today's fashions, popular sports and cartoon heroes, shiny wrappers from your favorite junk food, plastic foam packing peanuts, holed edges of computer paper, scraps of fabrics, and anything else you think says something about our times. You may find out something about yourself by the items you choose to collect. Arrange your selection onto wood or a stiff piece of cardboard in a collage and use white glue or a hot glue gun to adhere them. You may want to paint some or all of the items once they are glued down, or color certain areas with crayons.

Campbell's
BEEF BROTH
Campbell's
CHICKEN NOODLE
Campbell's
TOMATO
Campbell's
VEGETABLE

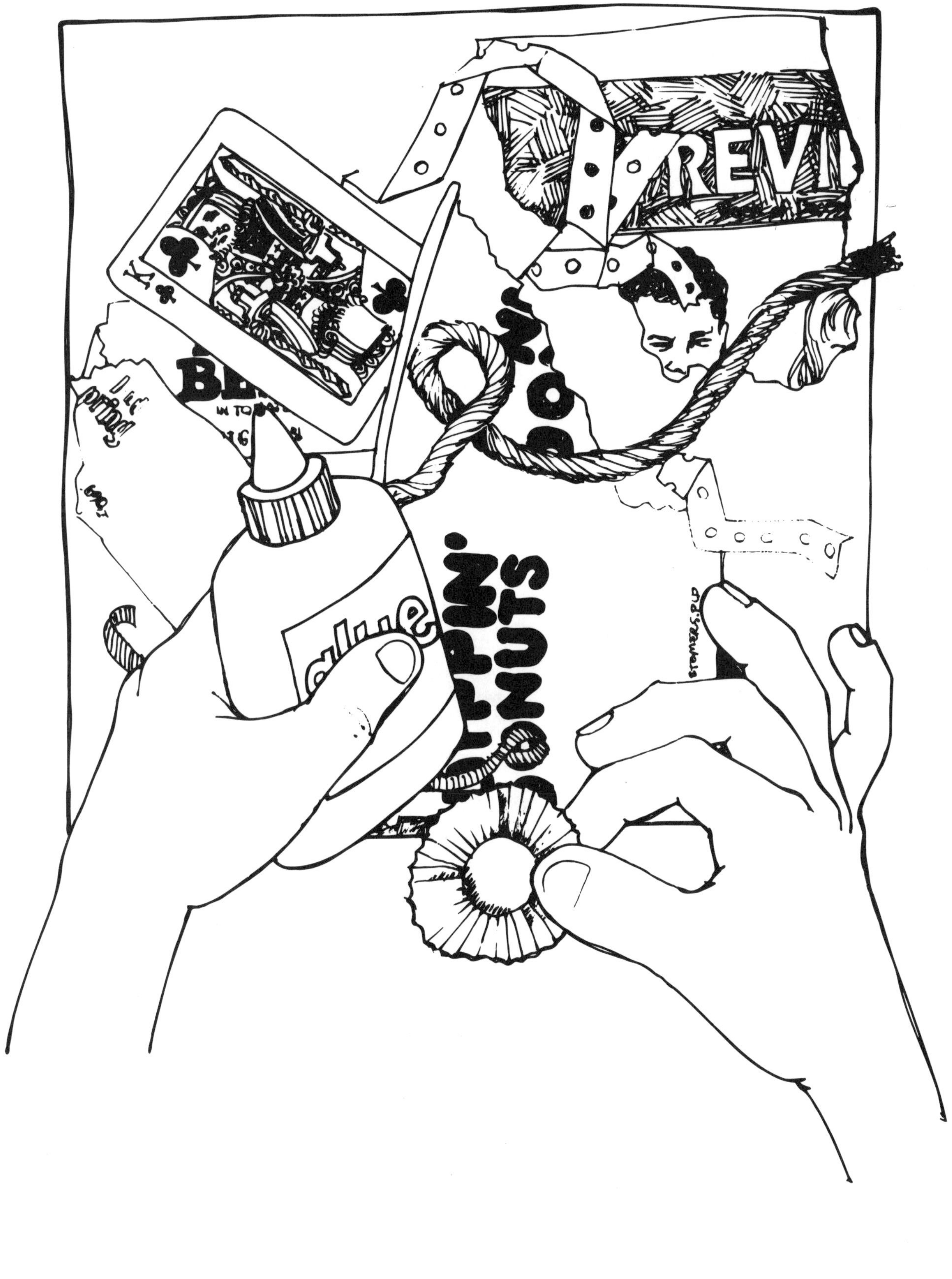
REVI
glue

What's Next?

Where will art go from here? No one can say for sure, but it seems a likely direction would be toward computerized art. Computers today create unbelievably complex images that seem to take us into a whole new reality with unlimited possibilities. Maybe someday we will be able to simply think images and emotions and they will appear on the screen in color. Perhaps art will become interactive. Maybe a totally new art form will be invented which combines images from our other senses—smell, taste, touch, and sound with our visual image. Who knows?

Activities and Projects

Imagine that you are an artist in the 21st century. Develop your own art movement. What is the name of your movement? What styles are you rebelling against? What is your medium? Do you use paint, or is your work entirely electronic? Write or illustrate your ideas about the new art of the next century.

A Final Word

Visual art is only one means by which people have expressed themselves and their beliefs throughout history. Music, dance, poetry, and other literature often echoed the same ideas which were influencing the art movements of a particular period. No one art form exists in a vacuum. While Monet painted beautiful Impressionist gardens to delight our eyes, Claude Debussy composed impressionist pieces such as "Clair de Lune" to delight our ears. The chants of Gregorian monks reflect the spiritual nature that is evident in much medieval art. The Baroque period of history produced both music and art with complicated and lavish embellishments. To better understand the people of any period of history, including ourselves, we need to explore as many art forms as possible. It is through these art forms that humans become human.

Bibliography

Batterberry, Ariane Ruskin. *The Pantheon Story of Art for Young People.* New York: Random House, 1964.

Boardman, John, ed. *The Oxford History of Modern Art.* Oxford: Oxford University Press, 1993.

Burrell, Roy. *The Greeks.* Oxford: Oxford University Press, 1990.

Connolly, Peter. *The Legend of Odysseus.* Oxford: Oxford University Press, 1986.

Coville, Bruce. *Prehistoric People.* New York: Doubleday, 1990.

Delluc, Brigitte. *Prehistoric Hunters.* Hertfordshire, England: Granada Pub., 1982.

Fremantle, Anne. *Age of Faith.* New York: Time, Inc., 1965.

Gardiner, Helen. *Art Through the Ages.* New York: Harcourt, Brace, Inc., 1959.

Hart, George. *Eyewitness Books Ancient Egypt.* New York: Alfred A. Knopf, 1990.

Hughes, Robert. "Behold the Stone Age." *Time,* Feb. 13, 1995.

Janson, H.W. and Anthony F. Janson. *History of Art for Young People.* New York: Harry N. Abrams, Inc., 1987.

Merriman, Nick, ed. *Early Humans.* New York: Alfred A. Knopf, Inc., 1989.

Plumb, J.H. *Horizon Book of the Renaissance.* New York: American Heritage Publishing Co, Inc., 1961.

Price, Christine. *Made in the Middle Ages.* New York: Dutton, 1961.

Putman, John. "The Search for Modern Humans." *National Geographic Magazine,* Oct. 1988, p.439.

Rockwell, Anne. *The Robber Baby: Stories From Ancient Greek Myths.* New York: Greenwillow Books, 1994.

Robinson, Charles Alexander. *The First Book of Ancient Greece.* New York: Franklin Watts, Inc., 1960.

Strong, Donald G. *The Classical World.* New York: McGraw Hill, 1965.

Vernus, Pascal. *Times of the Pharaohs.* St. Albans, Great Britain: Hart-Davis Educational Ltd., 1980.

Wood, Tim. *The Renaissance.* New York: Viking, 1993.